Grade 4

Skill Practice

TEACHING GUIDE

Copyright © 2007 Developmental Studies Center

All rights reserved. Except where otherwise noted, no part of this publication may be reproduced in whole or in part, or stored in a retrieval system, or transmitted in any form or by any means, electronic, mechanical, photocopying, recording, or otherwise, without the written permission of the publisher. For information regarding permissions, write to the Editorial Department at Developmental Studies Center.

Permission is granted to reproduce the blackline masters in this volume for classroom use only.

First edition published 2007.

Being a Writer is a trademark of Developmental Studies Center.

Developmental Studies Center
2000 Embarcadero, Suite 305
Oakland, CA 94606-5300
(800) 666-7270, fax: (510) 464-3670
www.devstu.org

ISBN: 978-1-59892-331-5

Printed in the United States of America

4 5 6 7 8 9 10 MLY 16 15 14 13 12

Table of Contents

Introduction i

Skill Practice Mini-lessons 1

Grammar and Usage 2

Recognize and use nouns and adjectives 2

Recognize and use verbs and adverbs 4

Recognize and use personal pronouns, possessive pronouns,
and possessive adjectives 6

Recognize and use prepositions and prepositional phrases 8

Recognize and divide run-on and very long sentences 10

Connect short, related sentences using appositives and participial phrases ... 12

Correctly use commonly misused words 14

Recognize subject-verb agreement with compound subjects 16

Recognize and consistently use past, present, and future verb tenses 18

Recognize and consistently use first, second, and third person
points of view 20

Identify and indent paragraphs 22

Recognize and use conjunctions to connect ideas 24

Punctuation and Capitalization 26

Use single and double quotation marks in speech and direct quotations 26

Use commas in a series 28

Capitalize proper nouns including ethnicities, languages, and religions 30

Cite books and magazine articles 32

Use parentheses 34

Use colons and semicolons 36

Review 38

Proofread for grammar, usage, punctuation, and capitalization 38

Blackline Masters 41

Grammar and Usage 42

Recognize and use nouns and adjectives 42

Recognize and use verbs and adverbs 43

Recognize and use personal pronouns, possessive pronouns,
and possessive adjectives 44

Recognize and use prepositions and prepositional phrases 45

Recognize and divide run-on and very long sentences 46

Connect short, related sentences using appositives and participial phrases ... 47

Correctly use commonly misused words 48

Recognize subject-verb agreement with compound subjects 49

continues

Table of Contents *continued*

Recognize and consistently use past, present, and future verb tenses 50

Recognize and consistently use first, second, and third person
points of view 51

Identify and indent paragraphs 52

Recognize and use conjunctions to connect ideas 53

Punctuation and Capitalization 54

Use single and double quotation marks in speech and direct quotation 54

Use commas in a series 55

Capitalize proper nouns including ethnicities, languages, and religions 56

Cite books and magazine articles 57

Use parentheses 58

Use colons and semicolons 59

Review 60

Proofread for grammar, usage, punctuation, and capitalization 60

Student Skill Practice Book Corrections 61

Grammar and Usage 62

Recognize and use nouns and adjectives 62

Recognize and use verbs and adverbs 64

Recognize and use personal pronouns, possessive pronouns,
and possessive adjectives 66

Recognize and use prepositions and prepositional phrases 68

Recognize and divide run-on and very long sentences 70

Connect short, related sentences using appositives and participial phrases ... 72

Correctly use commonly misused words 74

Recognize subject-verb agreement with compound subjects 76

Recognize and consistently use past, present, and future verb tenses 78

Recognize and consistently use first, second, and third person
points of view 80

Identify and indent paragraphs 82

Recognize and use conjunctions to connect ideas 84

Punctuation and Capitalization 86

Use single and double quotation marks in speech and direct quotation 86

Use commas in a series 88

Capitalize proper nouns including ethnicities, languages, and religions 90

Cite books and magazine articles 92

Use parentheses 94

Use colons and semicolons 96

Review 98

Proofread for grammar, usage, punctuation, and capitalization 98

Introduction

Welcome to the *Being a Writer Skill Practice Teaching Guide.* This component, along with the *Student Skill Practice Book,* supplements the *Being a Writer* core program by providing additional activities to help students practice the skills and conventions of written English. The skills selected for inclusion in this book are developmentally appropriate and consistent with prevailing standards of writing instruction at grade 4.

How to Use These Mini-lessons

You can use these 10- to 15-minute mini-lessons at any time to teach or review grammar, usage, punctuation, and capitalization skills with your class. Mini-lessons can reinforce skills taught in the core program, or they can teach or review additional skills required by your district or taught in prior years. The table on the following page shows which skills are included in these mini-lessons, if and where they are taught in the core program at this grade (marked as "Taught"), and which units in the core program lend themselves to continued practice of those skills (marked with an "X").

To teach these mini-lessons, you will need an overhead projector, transparencies of the blackline masters, extra blank transparencies, and overhead pens. Some mini-lessons also include optional steps requiring chart paper. The students may need separate sheets of paper to complete some of the activities.

While mastery of grammatical terms is not a primary goal of this program, it is helpful for students to hear these terms regularly when learning English language conventions. We encourage you to use proper grammatical terminology when discussing parts of speech and other conventions with your students.

Being a Writer™ • Grade Four i

Introduction

Grade 4 Skills

Taught = taught directly in the unit   **X** = appropriate to practice

Grammar and Usage	Personal Narrative	Fiction	Expository Nonfiction	Functional Nonfiction	Poetry
Recognize and use nouns and adjectives	X	Taught	X	X	X
Recognize and use verbs and adverbs	X	X	X	X	X
Recognize and use personal pronouns, possessive pronouns, and possessive adjectives	X	X	X	X	X
Recognize and use prepositions and prepositional phrases	X	X	X	X	X
Recognize and divide run-on and very long sentences	X	Taught	Taught	X	
Connect short, related sentences using appositives and participial phrases	X	X	X	X	
Correctly use commonly misused words	Taught	X	X	X	
Recognize subject-verb agreement with compound subjects	X	X	X	X	
Recognize and consistently use past, present, and future verb tenses	X	X	X	X	
Recognize and consistently use first, second, and third points of view	X	X	X	X	
Identify and indent paragraphs			X	X	
Recognize and use conjunctions to connect ideas			X	X	

Punctuation and Capitalization	Personal Narrative	Fiction	Expository Nonfiction	Functional Nonfiction	Poetry
Use single and double quotation marks in speech and direct quotations	X	Taught	X	X	
Use commas in a series	X	X	Taught	X	X
Use commas in direct quotations	X	X	X	X	
Capitalize proper nouns including ethnicities, languages, and religions	X	X	Taught	X	
Cite books and magazine articles			X	X	
Use parentheses			X	X	
Use colons and semicolons			X	X	

ii | Being a Writer™ • Grade Four

Skill Practice
Mini-lessons

Grammar and Usage

Skill: Recognize and use nouns and adjectives

Materials: Transparency of "People-watching" (page 42)
Overhead pens in two colors

Lesson:

1. Explain that the students will practice recognizing and using nouns and adjectives to help them in their writing. Explain that nouns and adjectives are kinds of words in the English language—a *noun* is a word for a person (or animal), place, or thing; an *adjective* is a word that describes a noun.

2. Show part A of "People-watching" on the overhead projector and read it aloud.

3. Model identifying and underlining a noun (such as *weekends*) and an adjective (such as *most*). Ask:

   Q *What other nouns do you see in this passage? What other adjectives do you see?*

   As the students respond, underline nouns in one color and adjectives in another on the transparency. (See "People-watching: Corrections" on the facing page.)

4. Think aloud and model adding an adjective to the passage (such as the word *hungry* before *pigeons*). Ask:

   Q *What other adjectives could we add to this passage?*

5. Read part B aloud. Use the students' suggestions to write a short passage that includes interesting nouns and adjectives. Underline nouns in one color and adjectives in another.

6. (Optional) Brainstorm adjectives as a class and record them on a chart labeled "Interesting Adjectives." Post the chart, add to it over time, and encourage the students to use the adjectives in their own writing.

7. (Optional) Ask the students to open to *Student Skill Practice Book* page 1. Read the directions aloud and have the students work individually or in pairs on the activity. For additional practice with this skill, assign the activities on pages 2–4 of the *Student Skill Practice Book*. (For corrections for these activities, see pages 62–63 of the *Skill Practice Teaching Guide*.)

2 | Being a Writer™ • Grade Four

Skill Practice Mini-lesson

Grammar and Usage: Recognize and use nouns and adjectives

People-watching: Corrections

A. **Nouns are underlined with a solid line and adjectives are underlined with a dotted line. Additional adjectives will vary. Suggestions are shown below.**

I like watching people in the park on most weekends. A man in a straw hat sells hot pretzels and cold sodas from his cart. Teenagers do wild tricks on skateboards. An elderly woman sprinkles crumbs on the grass for the _hungry_ pigeons. Parents push strollers and clutch the _sweaty_ hands of _excited_ toddlers. _Daring performers_ ~~Performers~~ sometimes gather to practice juggling balls, plates, and even swords.

B. **Check for the appropriate use of nouns and adjectives in the passage.**

Skill Practice Mini-lesson   Being a Writer™ • Grade Four | 3

Grammar and Usage

Skill: Recognize and use verbs and adverbs

Materials: Transparency of "Desert Kangaroo Rats" (page 43)
Overhead pens in two colors

Lesson:

1. Explain that the students will practice recognizing and using verbs and adverbs to help them in their writing. Explain that verbs and adverbs are kinds of words in the English language—a *verb* is a word that shows an action; an *adverb* is a word that tells more about a verb.

2. Show part A of "Desert Kangaroo Rats" on the overhead projector and read it aloud.

3. Model identifying and underlining a verb (such as *jumps*) and an adverb (such as *far*). Ask:

   Q *What other verbs do you see in this passage? What other adverbs do you see?*

   As the students respond, underline verbs in one color and adverbs in another on the transparency. (See "Desert Kangaroo Rats: Corrections" on the facing page.)

4. Think aloud and model adding an adverb to the passage (such as the word *loudly* before *drums* in "The rat drums its legs on the ground to communicate"). Ask:

   Q *What other adverbs could we add to this passage?*

5. Read part B aloud. Use the students' suggestions to write a short passage that includes interesting verbs and adverbs. Underline verbs in one color and adverbs in another.

6. (Optional) Brainstorm verbs and adverbs as a class and record them on charts labeled "Interesting Verbs" and "Interesting Adverbs." Post the charts and add to them over time. Encourage the students to use the verbs and adverbs in their own writing.

7. (Optional) Ask the students to open to *Student Skill Practice Book* page 5. Read the directions aloud and have the students work individually or in pairs on the activity. For additional practice with this skill, assign the activities on pages 6–8 of the *Student Skill Practice Book*. (For corrections for these activities, see pages 64–65 of the *Skill Practice Teaching Guide*.)

4 | Being a Writer™ • Grade Four | *Skill Practice Mini-lesson*

Grammar and Usage: Recognize and use verbs and adverbs

Desert Kangaroo Rats: Corrections

A. **Verbs are underlined with a solid line and adverbs are underlined with a dotted line. Additional adverbs will vary. Suggestions are shown below.**

The desert kangaroo rat got its name because it jumps far

on powerful back legs like a kangaroo. Those legs help the

loudly

rat in other ways too. The rat drums its legs on the ground

to communicate. If it finds a visitor in its hole, or burrow, it

energetically pounds the ground to tell the animal to leave.

On a quiet day, you can clearly hear the sound up to 150 feet

suddenly

away. When the desert kangaroo rat meets an enemy, such as a

rattlesnake, it uses its strong legs to kick sand in the attacker's face.

B. **Check for the appropriate use of verbs and adverbs in the passage.**

Skill Practice Mini-lesson

Being a Writer™ • Grade Four | 5

Grammar and Usage

Skill: Recognize and use personal pronouns, possessive pronouns, and possessive adjectives

Materials: Transparency of "Nightmare" (page 44)
Overhead pens in three colors

Lesson:

1. Explain that the students will practice recognizing and using personal pronouns, possessive pronouns, and possessive adjectives. Personal pronouns such as *I*, *she*, and *him* stand for a person or thing ("*I* have a dog"). Possessive pronouns such as *mine*, *yours*, and *hers* show ownership ("The dog is *mine*"). Possessive adjectives such as *my*, *her*, and *our* are adjectives that show ownership ("This is *my* dog").

2. Show part A of "Nightmare" on the overhead projector and read it aloud.

3. Model identifying and underlining a pronoun or possessive adjective (such as *I*). Ask:

   Q *Is [I] a personal pronoun, possessive pronoun, or possessive adjective?*

   Q *What other pronouns or possessive adjectives do you see in this passage? Is [our] a personal pronoun, possessive pronoun, or possessive adjective?*

   As the students respond, underline the personal pronouns in one color, the possessive pronouns in another color, and the possessive adjectives in a third color on the transparency. (See "Nightmare: Corrections" on the facing page.)

4. Read the first paragraph in part B aloud. Ask:

   Q *What pronoun or possessive adjective can we use to complete the second sentence?*

   As the students respond, fill in the blank and complete the sentence. Continue to fill in the remaining blanks to complete the passage.

5. Read part C aloud. Use the students' suggestions to write a short passage.

6. (Optional) For additional practice with this skill, have the students work individually or in pairs on the activities on pages 9–12 of the *Student Skill Practice Book*. (For corrections for these activities, see pages 66–67 of the *Skill Practice Teaching Guide*.)

6 | Being a Writer™ • Grade Four

Skill Practice Mini-lesson

Grammar and Usage: Recognize and use personal pronouns, possessive pronouns, and possessive adjectives

Nightmare: Corrections

A. **Personal pronouns are underlined with a solid line, possessive pronouns are underlined with a dotted line, and possessive adjectives are underlined with a double line.**

Last night I dreamed I forgot where our family lives. I entered the Smiths' house. Their son Marcus came out of his room, frowning. Mrs. Smith looked up from the book she was reading. The cat glared at me from its cushion. They all seemed surprised.

B. **The correct word is written in each blank.**

"I live here. This is ____my____ house," I said.

Mrs. Smith put ____her____ book down. "Honey, ____your____ parents must be wondering where you are. I'll take you home."

The cat yawned and licked ____its____ fur.

C. **Check for the appropriate use of possessive adjectives in the passage.**

Skill Practice Mini-lesson   Being a Writer™ • Grade Four | 7

Grammar and Usage

Skill: Recognize and use prepositions and prepositional phrases

Materials: Transparency of "Squirrel Skills" (page 45)
Overhead pens in two colors

Lesson:

1. Explain that the students will practice recognizing and using prepositions and prepositional phrases to help them in their writing. Explain that *prepositions* are words like *in*, *at*, *around*, and *under*, and that *prepositional phrases* are groups of words with a preposition in them that give more information about time (*in* the morning), location (*at* the board), direction (*around* the corner) or position (*under* the table) of something in a sentence.

2. Show part A of "Squirrel Skills" on the overhead projector and read it aloud.

3. Model identifying and underlining a preposition (such as *from*) and a prepositional phrase (such as *from their food*). Ask:

   Q *What other prepositions or prepositional phrases do you see in this passage?*

   As the students respond, underline the prepositions in one color and the prepositional phrases in another color. (See "Squirrel Skills: Corrections" on the facing page.)

4. Read part B aloud. Use the students' suggestions to write a few sentences that include prepositional phrases. Underline the prepositional phrases.

5. (Optional) Brainstorm prepositions as a class and record them on a chart labeled "Prepositions." Post the chart and add to it over time. Encourage the students to use a variety of prepositions in their own writing.

6. (Optional) Ask the students to open to *Student Skill Practice Book* page 13. Read the directions aloud and have the students work individually or in pairs on the activity. For additional practice with this skill, assign the activities on pages 14–16 of the *Student Skill Practice Book*. (For corrections for these activities, see pages 68–69 of the *Skill Practice Teaching Guide*.)

8 | Being a Writer™ • Grade Four

Skill Practice Mini-lesson

Grammar and Usage: Recognize and use prepositions and prepositional phrases

Squirrel Skills: Corrections

A. **Prepositions are underlined with a solid line and prepositional phrases are underlined with a dotted line.**

Squirrels work hard to keep others away from their food. A squirrel might dig several holes and only bury a nut in one of them. It might bury a nut and then pretend to bury another near the first one. It might bury a nut under a bush, or climb up a tree and store a nut in a nest, beyond the reach of many animals.

B. **Check for the appropriate use of prepositions and underlining of prepositional phrases in the sentences.**

Skill Practice Mini-lesson

Being a Writer™ • Grade Four | 9

Grammar and Usage

Skill: Recognize and divide run-on and very long sentences

Materials: Transparency of "Snakes" (page 46)
Overhead pen

Lesson:

1. Explain that the students will practice recognizing and correcting run-on and very long sentences to help them in their writing. Explain that *run-on* and *very long sentences* have two or more complete thoughts joined together without a connecting word or correct punctuation.

2. Show part A of "Snakes" on the overhead projector. Read it aloud. Ask:

   Q *What do you notice about this passage?*

   Explain that one way to fix run-on and very long sentences is to read the writing aloud and listen to where your voice naturally pauses. Reread the beginning of the passage, pausing after the word *snakes* and then continuing to the word *sizes*. Ask:

   Q *Where did you hear a pause in the words?*

   Model adding a period and capitalizing the beginning of the next sentence. Reread the new sentence to verify that it makes sense on its own.

3. Continue reading the passage and correcting the remaining run-on sentences. (See "Snakes: Corrections" on the facing page.)

4. Repeat with part B. Point out that the words *and*, *so*, and *then* are being used to join many thoughts together, creating one very long sentence where there should be multiple sentences.

5. (Optional) Ask the students to open to *Student Skill Practice Book* page 17. Read the directions aloud and have the students work individually or in pairs on the activity. For additional practice with this skill, assign the activities on pages 18–20 of the *Student Skill Practice Book*. (For corrections for these activities, see pages 70–71 of the *Skill Practice Teaching Guide*.)

10 │ Being a Writer™ • Grade Four

Skill Practice Mini-lesson

Grammar and Usage: Recognize and divide run-on and very long sentences

Snakes: Corrections

A. Corrections appear below.

There are more than two thousand kinds (species) of snakes. ~~they~~ **T** come in many sizes. **T** the Texas Slender Blind snake is only about five inches long. **I** it weighs about 0.1 ounces. **T** the Anaconda can grow as long as 33 feet. **I** it can weigh up to 550 pounds.

B. Corrections appear below.

Many species of snakes kill their prey by wrapping their long body around the animal. **T** ~~so~~ they slowly tighten their coils around the victim. **O** ~~then~~ once the animal is dead they swallow it whole. **T** ~~and~~ they prefer to swallow their prey head first. **A** ~~and a~~ snake that squeezes its prey to death is called a constrictor.

Skill Practice Mini-lesson   Being a Writer™ • Grade Four | **11**

Grammar and Usage

Skill: Connect short, related sentences using appositives and participial phrases

Materials: Transparency of "Sentence Pairs" (page 47)
Overhead pen

Lesson:

1. Explain that the students will practice combining short, related sentences into one longer sentence and dividing long sentences into shorter sentences. Point out that this practice will give them more flexibility in their own writing.

2. Show part A of "Sentence Pairs" on the overhead projector. Read the first sentence aloud. Ask:

   Q *How can we turn this sentence into two, shorter sentences?*

   As the students respond, write out the sentences. (See "Sentence Pairs: Corrections" on the facing page.)

3. Repeat with the next two sentences.

4. Read the first two sentences of part B aloud. Ask:

   Q *How can we combine these two sentences into one sentence?*

   As the students respond, write out the sentence. Continue the procedure with the remaining sentences.

5. (Optional) Ask the students to open to *Student Skill Practice Book* page 21. Read the directions aloud and have the students work individually or in pairs on the activity. For additional practice with this skill, assign the activities on pages 22–24 of the *Student Skill Practice Book*. (For corrections for these activities, see pages 72–73 of the *Skill Practice Teaching Guide*.)

12 | Being a Writer™ • Grade Four   *Skill Practice Mini-lesson*

Grammar and Usage: Connect short, related sentences using appositives and participial phrases

Sentence Pairs: Corrections

A. Corrections are shown below.

Miguel, a bookworm, reads for at least two hours every evening.

Miguel _is a bookworm._

Miguel _reads for at least two hours every evening._

Stonehenge, a prehistoric monument, was built around 3100 BC.

Stonehenge is a prehistoric monument.

Stonehenge was built around 3100 BC.

B. Corrections are shown below.

My neighbor is a nurse.

My neighbor works in the emergency ward.

My neighbor, a nurse, works in the emergency ward.

Gorillas are the largest and strongest of the apes.

Gorillas live in Africa.

Gorillas, the largest and strongest of the apes, live in Africa.

Skill Practice Mini-lesson

Being a Writer™ • Grade Four | 13

Grammar and Usage

Skill: Correctly use commonly misused words

Materials: Transparency of "Vacation Daze" (page 48)
Overhead pen

Lesson:

1. Explain that the students will practice finding and correcting commonly misused words to help them in their writing.

2. Show part A of "Vacation Daze" on the overhead projector and read it aloud.

3. Reread the first sentence and model identifying and correcting the commonly misused word *would*. Ask:

   Q *What other misused word[s] do you see in this passage? What word should we replace it with?*

4. As the students respond, cross out any misused word and write the correct word above it. (See "Vacation Daze: Corrections" on the facing page.)

5. Read part B aloud. Use the students' suggestions to write a short passage using at least three commonly misused words correctly.

6. (Optional) Ask the students to open to *Student Skill Practice Book* page 25. Read the directions aloud and have the students work individually or in pairs on the activity. For additional practice with this skill, assign the activities on pages 26–28 of the *Student Skill Practice Book*. (For corrections for these activities, see pages 74–75 of the *Skill Practice Teaching Guide*.)

14 | Being a Writer™ • Grade Four

Skill Practice Mini-lesson

Grammar and Usage: Correctly use commonly misused words

Vacation Daze: Corrections

A.   Corrections are shown below.

       I thought I ~~wood~~ *would* love vacation. I thought it would be ~~grate~~ *great*
~~two~~ *to* have a ~~brake~~ *break* from memorizing facts and ~~righting~~ *writing* till my arm
drops off. But I never ~~guest~~ *guessed* I could be so ~~board~~ *bored*. I walk ~~buy~~ *by* the
~~creak~~ *creek* near our house, counting the ~~ours~~ *hours* and days until school
starts. I still have another ~~weak~~ *week* ~~too~~ *to* wait. Can you ~~here~~ *hear* my groan?
I have no ~~patients~~ *patience* left! I'm ~~threw~~ *through* with this vacation!

B.   Check for the correct use of commonly misused words in the passage.

Skill Practice Mini-lesson   Being a Writer™ • Grade Four | **15**

Grammar and Usage

Skill: Recognize subject-verb agreement with compound subjects

Materials: Transparency of "Making Monsters" (page 49)
Overhead pen

Lesson:

1. Show part A of "Making Monsters" and read it aloud. Reread the first sentence and model identifying and underlining a verb (such as *make*). Ask:

   Q *What other verbs to do you see in the passage?*

   As the students respond, underline the remaining verbs in the passage. (See "Making Monsters: Corrections" on the facing page.)

2. Read part B aloud. Model identifying an incorrect verb (such as *twists*) and writing the correct verb above it. Ask:

   Q *What other verbs need to be corrected in this passage?*

   As the students respond, cross out the incorrect verbs and write the correct verbs above them on the transparency.

3. Read part C aloud. Ask:

   Q *What verbs need to be corrected in this passage?*

   As the students respond, cross out the incorrect verbs and write the correct verbs above them.

4. (Optional) Ask the students to open to *Student Skill Practice Book* page 29. Read the directions aloud and have the students work individually or in pairs on the activity. For additional practice with this skill, assign the activities on pages 30–32 of the *Student Skill Practice Book*. (For corrections for these activities, see pages 76–77 of the *Skill Practice Teaching Guide*.)

16 | Being a Writer™ • Grade Four   *Skill Practice Mini-lesson*

Grammar and Usage: Recognize subject-verb agreement with compound subjects

Making Monsters: Corrections

A. Verbs are underlined below.

My friends and I <u>make</u> papier-mâché monsters. Cara <u>twists</u> wire into shapes. Tod <u>makes</u> the paste. I <u>tear</u> strips of newspaper. Binh <u>puts</u> paste on them and <u>plasters</u> them onto the wire.

B. All verbs are underlined, and necessary corrections to verbs are shown below.

My friends and I <u>make</u> papier-mâché monsters. Cara and Doug ~~<u>twists</u>~~ *twist* wire into shapes. Tod and Amy ~~<u>makes</u>~~ *make* the paste. Rob and I <u>tear</u> strips of newspaper. Binh and Leah ~~<u>puts</u>~~ *put* paste on them and ~~<u>plasters</u>~~ *plaster* them onto the wire.

C. Corrections to verbs are shown below.

We ~~waits~~ *wait* for it to dry. Later, we ~~decorates~~ *decorate* it. Rob and Tod ~~paints~~ *paint* it. Binh ~~glue~~ *glues* on eyeballs and antennae. Cara, Doug, and Amy ~~gives~~ *give* advice. I ~~tells~~ *tell* silly monster jokes.

Skill Practice Mini-lesson   Being a Writer™ • Grade Four | **17**

Grammar and Usage

Skill: Recognize and consistently use past, present, and future verb tenses

Materials: Transparency of "Refuge or Dump?" (page 50)
Overhead pen

Lesson:

1. Explain that the students will practice using past, present, and future verb tenses to help them in their writing. Explain that *past tense* verbs happen in the past (such as *ran*), *present tense* verbs happen in the present (*run*), and *future tense* verbs happen in the future (*will run*).

2. Show part A of "Refuge or Dump?" on the overhead projector and read it aloud.

3. Model identifying the tense of a verb (such as *was*) and underlining it. Ask:

   Q *What other verbs do you see in this passage? What tense is that verb?*

   As the students respond, underline the verbs and note the tense above them. (See "Refuge or Dump? Corrections" on the facing page.)

4. Read part B aloud. Use the students' suggestions to write three short paragraphs using past, present, and future verb tenses. Underline the verbs in each paragraph.

5. (Optional) Brainstorm verbs as a class and record the past, present, and future tense of each on a chart labeled "Past, Present, and Future Verb Tenses." Post the chart and add to it over time. Encourage the students to use the verb tenses in their own writing.

6. (Optional) Ask the students to open to *Student Skill Practice Book* page 33. Read the directions aloud and have the students work individually or in pairs on the activity. For additional practice with this skill, assign the activities on pages 34–36 of the *Student Skill Practice Book*. (For corrections for these activities, see pages 78–79 of the *Skill Practice Teaching Guide*.)

18 | Being a Writer™ • Grade Four   *Skill Practice Mini-lesson*

Grammar and Usage: Recognize and consistently use past, present, and future verb tenses

Refuge or Dump? Corrections

A.   Verbs are underlined and marked to signify past (*pa*), present (*pr*), or future (*f*) tense.

    The Potomac River <u>was</u> [pa] once part of a wilderness where a group of Native American tribes <u>lived</u> [pa]. After Europeans <u>took over</u> [pa] the area, the river <u>became</u> [pa] famous for its nearness to our nation's capital, Washington, DC.

    Today the river <u>has</u> [pr] lots of trash in it. The good news <u>is</u> [pr] that every spring, thousands of citizen volunteers <u>clean</u> [pr] it up. Young and old alike <u>participate</u> [pr].

    What <u>will happen</u> [f] to the Potomac? Maybe people <u>will dump</u> [f] so much garbage in it that cleanup <u>will become</u> [f] difficult. Or maybe they <u>will stop</u> [f] polluting and the river <u>will be</u> [f] trash-free once more.

B.   Check appropriate use of verb tense in the paragraphs.

Skill Practice Mini-lesson   Being a Writer™ • Grade Four | 19

Grammar and Usage

Skill: Recognize and consistently use first, second, and third person points of view

Materials: Transparency of "Life on Mars" (page 51)
Overhead pen

Lesson:

1. Explain that the *point of view* of a piece of writing tells the reader who is talking. There are three main points of view in writing: *first, second,* and *third person.*

2. Write the following three sentences on the board: *My name is Blanca and I ride horses. Her name is Blanca and she rides horses. Your name is Blanca and you ride horses.* Ask:

   Q (Point to the first sentence.) *Who is talking, or who is the narrator, in this sentence?*

   Point out that Blanca is the narrator, and that whenever there is an "I" narrator, the piece is written from the *first person point of view.* Ask:

   Q (Point to the second sentence.) *Who is the narrator in this sentence?*

   Point out that the reader cannot tell who the narrator is. When there is no "I" telling the story, the piece is written from the *third person point of view.* Ask:

   Q (Point to the third sentence.) *Who is the narrator in this sentence?*

   Explain that, like the third person point of view, the reader cannot tell who the narrator is. When the pronoun "you" is used, the piece is written from the *second person point of view*; this point of view is less common than the first and third.

3. Show part A of "Life on Mars" on the overhead projector and read it aloud. Ask:

   Q *From what point of view is the passage written? How can you tell?*

4. Use the students' suggestions to write the new passages in parts B and C.

5. (Optional) Ask the students to open to *Student Skill Practice Book* page 37. Read the directions aloud and have the students work individually or in pairs on the activity. For additional practice with this skill, assign the activities on pages 38–40 of the *Student Skill Practice Book.* (For corrections for these activities, see pages 80–81 of the *Skill Practice Teaching Guide.*)

20 | Being a Writer™ • Grade Four   *Skill Practice Mini-lesson*

Grammar and Usage: Recognize and consistently use first, second, and third person points of view

Life on Mars: Corrections

A.   The first passage is written from the third person point of view.

B.   Below is the passage rewritten from the first person point of view.

A finger tapped my shoulder. I turned over and mumbled sleepily. It was too early to get up! I reached to pat my mother's hand—only to touch cold steel. I bolted upright. I stared at the little robot scurrying out my bedroom door; then I flopped back down on my bed.

Below is the passage rewritten from the second person point of view.

A finger tapped your shoulder. You turned over and mumbled sleepily. It was too early to get up! You reached up to pat your mother's hand—only to touch cold steel. You bolted upright. You stared at the little robot scurrying out your bedroom door; then you flopped back down on your bed.

C.   Check the passage for consistent point of view.

Skill Practice Mini-lesson   Being a Writer™ • Grade Four   21

Grammar and Usage

Skill: Identify and indent paragraphs

Materials: Transparency of "Tadpoles" (page 52)
              Overhead pen

Lesson:

1. Explain that the students will practice indenting paragraphs to help them in their writing. Explain that a *paragraph* is a group of sentences that share a common topic or main idea. The first sentence of a paragraph is *indented*, or starts a few spaces to the right of the left margin.

2. Show part A of "Tadpoles" on the overhead projector, and read the first paragraph aloud. Ask:

   Q *What is the main idea of this paragraph?*

   Repeat with the second paragraph. Point out that each paragraph begins with a new idea, and that each paragraph is indented. (See "Tadpoles: Corrections" on the facing page.)

3. Read part B aloud. Ask:

   Q *Where should a new paragraph begin?*

   As the students respond, insert a paragraph symbol (¶) wherever a new paragraph should start. Reread each paragraph to make sure all of the sentences share a common topic or main idea.

4. (Optional) Ask the students to open to *Student Skill Practice Book* page 41. Read the directions aloud and have the students work individually or in pairs on the activity. For additional practice with this skill, assign the activities on pages 42–44 of the *Student Skill Practice Book*. (For corrections for these activities, see pages 82–83 of the *Skill Practice Teaching Guide*.)

22 | Being a Writer™ • Grade Four   *Skill Practice Mini-lesson*

Grammar and Usage: Identify and indent paragraphs

Tadpoles: Corrections

A. **The main idea of each paragraph is given below.**

Tadpoles are the young of toads and frogs. They hatch from eggs and live in the water. If tadpoles can avoid being eaten by other animals, they can mature into adult frogs or toads.

Main idea: *Tadpoles are the young of frogs and toads.*

A tadpole goes through several stages of growth. After it hatches, it looks like a little black comma with gills. Skin grows over the gills. Legs appear. Lungs grow and the tail shrinks.

Main idea: *Tadpoles go through several stages of growth.*

B. **The paragraph symbol (¶) is shown where it makes sense to begin a new paragraph.**

¶
Tadpoles are fun pets. You can watch as they turn into frogs. You can even play scientist, keeping a notebook and noting ¶
observations. Tadpoles are also a responsibility. You need to create a healthy home for them. If you keep them after they've grown, you'll need to create a new habitat for them.

Skill Practice Mini-lesson   Being a Writer™ • Grade Four | 23

Grammar and Usage

Skill: Recognize and use conjunctions to connect ideas

Materials: Transparency of "Get Connected" (page 53)
Overhead pen

Lesson:

1. Show part A of "Get Connected" on the overhead projector and read the first paragraph aloud. Ask:

   Q *What do you notice about the underlined words in the passage?*

   Point out that all of the underlined words are called *conjunctions*. Conjunctions connect ideas or show relationships among them.

2. Read part B aloud. Reread the first two sentences and model joining them together by crossing out unnecessary words and adding a conjunction and any necessary punctuation. Ask:

   Q *What other ideas can be connected using a conjunction?*

   As the students respond, connect related ideas using conjunctions throughout the rest of the passage. (See "Get Connected: Corrections" on the facing page.)

3. (Optional) Ask the students to open to *Student Skill Practice Book* page 45. Read the directions aloud and have the students work individually or in pairs on the activity. For additional practice with this skill, assign the activities on pages 46–48 of the *Student Skill Practice Book*. (For corrections for these activities, see pages 84–85 of the *Skill Practice Teaching Guide*.)

24 | Being a Writer™ • Grade Four · *Skill Practice Mini-lesson*

Grammar and Usage: Recognize and use conjunctions to connect ideas

Get Connected: Corrections

A. **The underlined words in the paragraph below are all conjunctions, or words that connect or show relationships among ideas.**

Babies have over 100 more bones than adults, <u>so</u> where do those bones go? <u>Since</u> they don't dissolve <u>or</u> evaporate, we must assume they grow together, <u>and</u>, in fact, they do. Many "bones" in a baby's body are made of cartilage. <u>As</u> the baby grows, the material that makes the hard bones of adults replaces the cartilage.

B. **Examples of ways to use conjunctions in the paragraph are given below.**

Although your ~~Your~~ skeleton is light~~,~~ *, it is also* ~~Your skeleton is~~ strong. To keep it strong, you have to take care of your bones. Being active can strengthen bones~~.~~ *, and you* ~~You~~ can dance *or* ~~to be active. You can~~ play sports to be active. Eating foods with calcium also strengthens bones. People think only dairy products have calcium~~.~~ *, but sardines* ~~Sardines~~, broccoli, tofu, and greens also contain calcium. Taking care of your bones now will help you be a healthy, active adult.

Skill Practice Mini-lesson   Being a Writer™ • Grade Four | 25

Punctuation and Capitalization

Skill: Use single and double quotation marks in speech and direct quotations

Materials: Transparency of "Great Grandma Remembers" (page 54)
              Overhead pen

Lesson:

1. Explain that the students will practice using single and double quotation marks to help them in their writing. Explain that *double quotation marks* are used to show the words a character is speaking, and *single quotation marks* are used inside double quotation marks to show when a character is repeating words that have been said before.

2. Show part A of "Great Grandma Remembers" on the overhead projector and read it aloud. Reread the first paragraph. Explain that double quotation marks are used around *We had fun expressions* and *We said 'clam' when we meant 'dollar'* to show that Great Grandma is speaking. Single quotation marks are used around the words *clam* and *dollar* to show that she is repeating words that have been spoken before.

3. Read the next line of the dialogue and model inserting double quotation marks around the word *weird*. Ask:

   Q *Where else are double quotation marks needed in this line?*

4. Continue reading the remaining lines of the dialogue. After each line, ask:

   Q *Where are quotation marks needed? Do we use double or single quotation marks?*

   As the students respond, place quotation marks wherever appropriate. (See "Great Grandma Remembers: Corrections" on the facing page.)

5. Read part B aloud. Use the students' suggestions to write a brief dialogue using double and single quotation marks.

6. (Optional) Ask the students to open to *Student Skill Practice Book* page 49. Read the directions aloud and have the students work individually or in pairs on the activity. For additional practice with this skill, assign the activities on pages 50–52 of the *Student Skill Practice Book*. (For corrections for these activities, see pages 86–87 of the *Skill Practice Teaching Guide*.)

26 | Being a Writer™ • Grade Four   *Skill Practice Mini-lesson*

Punctuation and Capitalization: Use single and double quotation marks in speech and direct quotations

Great Grandma Remembers: Corrections

A.   Correct use of single and double quotation marks is shown below.

The last time I visited Great Grandma, she described the slang terms she used in the old days.

"We had fun expressions," she explained. "We said 'clam' when we meant 'dollar.'"

"Weird," I said. "You used a sea animal to describe money."

"We used lots of animal words," she said. "Instead of saying, 'I think you're great,' we said, 'You're the cat's pajamas.' If we liked something, we said, 'That's just ducky.' We had other fun expressions too. 'Scram' meant 'leave quickly.' 'I've got the heebie-jeebies' meant 'I'm nervous.'"

"That's just ducky," I said. "Great Grandma, you're the cat's pajamas. But I should scram. I promised Dad I'd give him the clam I owe him before 4:00 PM. If I'm late, I'll get the heebie-jeebies."

B.   Check for the appropriate use of single and double quotation marks in the dialogue.

Skill Practice Mini-lesson   Being a Writer™ • Grade Four | 27

Punctuation and Capitalization

Skill: Use commas in a series

Materials: Transparency of "Dark Chocolate, Anyone?" (page 55)
Overhead pen

Lesson:

1. Explain that the students will practice using commas in a series to help them in their writing. Explain that a *series* is a list of three or more things, and commas are needed to separate the things in the list.

2. Show part A of "Dark Chocolate, Anyone?" on the overhead projector and read the first paragraph aloud. Ask:

   Q *What do you notice about how commas are used in this paragraph?*

   Point out that in a series of three or more things, the word *and* or *or* is used after the final comma. Read the second paragraph aloud; then ask:

   Q *What series do you see in this passage? Where in that series should we add commas?*

   As the students respond, add commas wherever appropriate. (See "Dark Chocolate, Anyone? Corrections" on the facing page.)

3. Read part B aloud. Use the students' suggestions to write a paragraph with series in it. (Possible topics include favorite foods and healthy habits.)

4. (Optional) Write a shared paragraph about a topic your class has studied this year. Have the students help you insert commas and the word *and* in series within the paragraph as appropriate.

5. (Optional) Ask the students to open to *Student Skill Practice Book* page 53. Read the directions aloud and have the students work individually or in pairs on the activity. For additional practice with this skill, assign the activities on pages 54–56 of the *Student Skill Practice Book*. (For corrections for these activities, see pages 88–89 of the *Skill Practice Teaching Guide*.)

28 | Being a Writer™ • Grade Four *Skill Practice Mini-lesson*

Punctuation and Capitalization: Use commas in a series

Dark Chocolate, Anyone? Corrections

A. Correct use of commas in the second paragraph of the passage is shown below.

Eating too much chocolate can contribute to cavities, weight gain, and diabetes. But some chocolate may actually be good for you. Dark chocolate has antioxidants. These may help prevent heart disease, Alzheimer's disease, and cancer. Keep in mind that milk chocolate, white chocolate, and many chocolate sauces don't have antioxidants. And it's unwise to stuff yourself on *any* sweets— even if they have healing properties!

B. Check for the appropriate use of commas in a series in the sentences.

Skill Practice Mini-lesson

Punctuation and Capitalization

Skill: Capitalize proper nouns including ethnicities, languages, and religions

Materials: Transparency of "Almanac Facts" (page 56)
Overhead pen

Lesson:

1. Explain that the students will practice capitalizing proper nouns including *ethnicities, languages,* and *religions.*

2. Show part A of "Almanac Facts" and read it aloud. Reread the first sentence and model capitalizing *russia* and *russian.* Ask:

   Q *What other words do you see that need to be capitalized?*

   As the students respond, cross out the lower case letters and write the capital letter above the word. (See "Almanac Facts: Corrections" on the facing page.)

3. Read part B aloud. Have students refer to the corrected passage in part A. Ask:

   Q *What types of words in the passage need to be capitalized?*

   Q *What other types of words (that aren't in the passage) need to be capitalized?*

   As students respond, write the different types of proper nouns in the box. Students might need help identifying *ethnicities* as a category.

4. Read part C aloud. Use the students' suggestions to list proper nouns that fit in the selected categories.

5. (Optional) Ask the students to open to *Student Skill Practice Book* page 57. Read the directions aloud and have the students work individually or in pairs on the activity. For additional practice with this skill, assign the activities on pages 58–60 of the *Student Skill Practice Book.* (For corrections for these activities, see pages 90–91 of the *Skill Practice Teaching Guide.*)

30 | Being a Writer™ • Grade Four

Skill Practice Mini-lesson

Punctuation and Capitalization: Capitalize proper nouns including ethnicities, languages, and religions

Almanac Facts: Corrections

A.   Corrections are shown below.

    R
russia is the world's largest country. It spans 11 time zones and

                                            R
two continents. The country's official language is russian. One of

                          R   *O*
the religions practiced there is russian orthodox.

    C
chile is the world's longest country. It's 2,700 miles long (the

                     S *F*   *M*
same distance as a trip from san francisco to manhattan). It's about

          C   *C*   *S*
twice the size of california. chile's official language is spanish. One

        C   *R*   *C*
religion that chileans practice is roman catholicism.

B.   Types of proper nouns in the passage are shown below.

- names of languages
- names of religions
- names of countries

- names of states
- names of cities
- names of ethnicities
  or nationalities

C.   Check for appropriate examples of the selected types of proper nouns.

Skill Practice Mini-lesson

Punctuation and Capitalization

Skill: Cite books and magazine articles*

Materials: Transparency of "Book Citations" (page 57)
Nonfiction book with a bibliography
Overhead pen

Lesson:

1. Explain that the students will practice writing book citations to help them in their writing. Show the students the bibliography in the back of a nonfiction book. Explain that when authors use other published work to get information for their own books they have to *cite* (give credit to) the resources they used. Explain that the *citations* are often found in a *bibliography*.

2. Show part A of "Book Citations" on the overhead projector and read it aloud. Ask:

   Q *What information do all of these book citations have in common?*

3. Explain that *book citations* always contain specific information, written in a specific order, using specific punctuation, as shown. Direct the students' attention to the incomplete citation. Ask:

   Q *What information needs to go [before the author's first name]?*

   As the students respond, fill in the first blank. Repeat the procedure to fill in the remaining blanks. As you write, point out the punctuation used to separate each part of the citation. (Note that italicized text would be underlined if handwritten.) If the students struggle, redirect them to the sample citations. (See "Book Citations: Corrections" on the facing page.)

4. Read part B aloud. Use the students' suggestions to write three book citations using books available in the classroom (avoid using text books).

5. (Optional) Ask the students to open to *Student Skill Practice Book* page 61. Read the directions aloud and have the students work individually or in pairs on the activity. For additional practice with this skill, assign the activities on pages 62–64 of the *Student Skill Practice Book*. (For corrections for these activities, see pages 92–93 of the *Skill Practice Teaching Guide*.)

* Students practice citing magazine articles in the *Student Skill Practice Book* (pages 63–64).

32 | Being a Writer™ • Grade Four   *Skill Practice Mini-lesson*

Punctuation and Capitalization: Cite books and magazine articles

Book Citations: Corrections

A. **The completed model for book citations is shown below.**

Author's last name, _Author's First name_ .

Book title in italics . _City where published_ ,

_____State_____: Publisher, _Copyright year_ .

B. **Check for the correct order of information and the correct use of punctuation and capitalization in the citations.**

Skill Practice Mini-lesson   Being a Writer™ • Grade Four | 33

Punctuation and Capitalization

Skill: Use parentheses

Materials: Transparency of "Sacagawea" (page 58)
Overhead pen

Lesson:

1. Explain that the students will practice using parentheses to help them in their writing. Explain that parentheses can be used to set apart dates or extra information, or to define words. Explain that information inside the parentheses can be taken out of the sentence, and the sentence will still make sense.

2. Show part A of "Sacagawea" on the overhead projector and read it aloud. Ask:

   Q *How are parentheses used in the first paragraph of the passage?*

3. Read part B aloud. Model identifying information that could be set apart using parentheses (for example *whose name means "Bird Woman"*). As you write the parentheses, explain that this information tells more about Sacagawea, but it is not necessary for the sentence to make sense. Ask:

   Q *What other information do you see that can be set apart using parentheses?*

   As the students respond, add parentheses where appropriate. (See "Sacagawea: Corrections" on the facing page.)

4. Read part C aloud. Use the students' suggestions to write a short passage that includes the use of parentheses.

5. (Optional) Ask the students to open to *Student Skill Practice Book* page 65. Read the directions aloud and have the students work individually or in pairs on the activity. For additional practice with this skill, assign the activities on pages 66–68 of the *Student Skill Practice Book*. (For corrections for these activities, see pages 94–95 of the *Skill Practice Teaching Guide*.)

34 | Being a Writer™ • Grade Four   *Skill Practice Mini-lesson*

Punctuation and Capitalization: Use parentheses

Sacagawea: Corrections

B. **Correct use of parentheses in the second paragraph of the passage is shown below.**

Sacagawea(whose name means "Bird Woman")was born in 1789 or 1790(the exact year is unknown). Most people believe she died in 1812.(Some think she lived until 1884.)She was from the Shoshone(Sho-SHO-nee)tribe. She had two children, Jean Baptiste(1805–1866)and Lisette(1812–?).

C. **Check for the appropriate use of parentheses in the passage.**

Skill Practice Mini-lesson   Being a Writer™ • Grade Four | **35**

Punctuation and Capitalization

Skill: Use colons and semicolons

Materials: Transparency of "Camp Is Boring" (page 59)
Overhead pen

Lesson:

1. Explain that the students will practice using colons and semicolons to help them in their writing. Write a colon and a semicolon on the board and identify which is which. Explain that colons and semicolons are used for different purposes in writing.

2. Show part A of "Camp Is Boring" on the overhead projector and read the first letter aloud. Ask:

    Q *Where do you see colons being used in this letter?*

    Explain that a colon can be used after the greeting in a letter, before starting a list, and when writing the time.

3. Read the second letter aloud. Ask:

    Q *Where do we need to add colons to this letter?*

    As the students respond, add colons to the letter wherever appropriate. (See "Camp Is Boring: Corrections" on the facing page.)

4. Read part B aloud. Model finding a sentence containing a conjunction. Explain that another way to join the two thoughts in the sentence is to use a semicolon. Model crossing out the conjunction and then inserting a semicolon. Ask:

    Q *Where else can we use a semicolon instead of a comma and conjunction?*

    As the students respond, add semicolons to the passage wherever appropriate.

5. (Optional) Ask the students to open to *Student Skill Practice Book* page 69. Read the directions aloud and have the students work individually or in pairs on the activity. For additional practice with this skill, assign the activities on pages 70–72 of the *Student Skill Practice Book*. (For corrections for these activities, see pages 96–97 of the *Skill Practice Teaching Guide*.)

36 | Being a Writer™ • Grade Four   *Skill Practice Mini-lesson*

Punctuation and Capitalization: Use colons and semicolons

Camp Is Boring: Corrections

A. Corrections for the second letter are shown below.

Dear Mollie:

You only arrived yesterday at 9:00 a.m. Wait two days; then call us. If you're still bored, we'll come.

Love,

Mom and Dad

B. Conjunctions have been replaced with semicolons in the sentence below.

Mollie called home two days later. "Guess what?" she said. "Yesterday I saw a bear; when we were on a hike. I'm not bored anymore; so don't come get me!"

Skill Practice Mini-lesson   Being a Writer™ • Grade Four | 37

Review

Skill: Proofread for grammar, usage, punctuation, and capitalization

Materials: Transparency of "The Okapi" (page 60)
         Overhead pen

Lesson:

1. Explain that the students will review some of the skills they have practiced in previous lessons.

2. Show part A of "The Okapi" on the overhead projector and read it aloud. Ask:

    Q *What do you notice?*

    Point out that the passage includes many errors.

3. Model finding the first few errors; then ask:

    Q *What other errors do you notice? What should we do to fix that error?*

    As the students respond, make corrections on the transparency using the editing marks you have established with your class. (See "The Okapi: Corrections" on the facing page.)

4. Read part B aloud. Use the students' suggestions to write a passage about something they have learned about recently. Stop to have the students explain why certain punctuation, capitalization, or word forms are needed.

5. (Optional) Have the students write their own passages. Have them work in pairs to read each other's passages, search for errors, and correct them.

6. (Optional) Ask the students to open to *Student Skill Practice Book* page 73. Read the directions aloud and have the students work individually or in pairs on the activity. For additional practice with this skill, assign the activities on pages 74–76 of the *Student Skill Practice Book*. (For corrections for these activities, see pages 98–99 of the *Skill Practice Teaching Guide*.)

38 | Being a Writer™ • Grade Four   *Skill Practice Mini-lesson*

Review: Proofread for grammar, usage, punctuation, and capitalization

The Okapi: Corrections

A.   Corrections are given below. Some answers may vary.

Have you heard of a creature that looks like a giraffe, donkey,

anteater, zebra, and antelope? Before the early 1900s, the okapi

(oh-COP-ee) was known only to the natives of the ~~i~~turi ~~r~~ainforest in
(I) (R)

~~a~~frica. Many ~~e~~uropeans who ~~herd tails~~ *heard tales* of the animal thought it ~~were~~ *was*
(A) (E)

a mythical creature like the unicorn~~.~~ *, but they* ~~They~~ were proven wrong.

~~sir~~ ~~harry~~ ~~johnston~~, ~~was~~ a ~~british~~ explorer, ~~Sir Harry Johnston~~
(S) (H) (J) (B)

was determined to find the truth about the elusive creature.

In 1899 he travel~~s~~ *ed* into the Congo ~~wear~~ *where* he heard stories and

was shown okapi's skulls and skins. In 1901, using Johnston's

information, the Zoological Society of London announced the

discovery of a new species of forest giraffe. It ~~will be~~ *was* given the

scientific name *Okapia Johnstoni*.

B.   Check for the appropriate use of the practiced skills in the passage.

Skill Practice Mini-lesson   Being a Writer™ • Grade Four | **39**

Blackline Masters

Grammar and Usage: Recognize and use nouns and adjectives

People-watching

A. **Read the passage below. Underline the nouns in one color and the adjectives in another. Add a few adjectives to the passage.**

I like watching people in the park on most weekends. A man in a straw hat sells hot pretzels and cold sodas from his cart. Teenagers do wild tricks on skateboards. An elderly woman sprinkles crumbs on the grass for the pigeons. Parents push strollers and clutch the hands of toddlers. Performers sometimes gather to practice juggling balls, plates, and even swords.

B. **Write a short passage using interesting nouns and adjectives. Underline the nouns in one color and the adjectives in another.**

42 Being a Writer™

© Developmental Studies Center

Grammar and Usage: Recognize and use verbs and adverbs

Desert Kangaroo Rats

A. **Read the passage below. Underline the verbs in one color and the adverbs in another. Add a few adverbs to the passage.**

The desert kangaroo rat got its name because it jumps far on powerful back legs like a kangaroo. Those legs help the rat in other ways too. The rat drums its legs on the ground to communicate. If it finds a visitor in its hole, or burrow, it energetically pounds the ground to tell the animal to leave. On a quiet day, you can clearly hear the sound up to 150 feet away. When the desert kangaroo rat meets an enemy, such as a rattlesnake, it uses its strong legs to kick sand in the attacker's face.

B. **Write a short passage using interesting verbs and adverbs. Underline the verbs in one color and the adverbs in another.**

© Developmental Studies Center

Being a Writer™ | **43**

Grammar and Usage: Recognize and use personal pronouns, possessive pronouns, and possessive adjectives

Nightmare

A. **Read the passage below. Underline personal pronouns in one color, possessive pronouns in another color, and possessive adjectives in a third color.**

Last night I dreamed I forgot where our family lives. I entered the Smiths' house. Their son Marcus came out of his room, frowning. Mrs. Smith looked up from the book she was reading. The cat glared at me from its cushion. They all seemed surprised.

B. **Read the passage below. Write the correct word in each blank.**

"I live here. This is _____ house," I said.

Mrs. Smith put _____ book down. "Honey, _____ parents must be wondering where you are. I'll take you home."

The cat yawned and licked _____ fur.

C. **Write a short passage using at least three of the possessive adjectives below.**

my   your   her   his   our   their   its

44 | Being a Writer™

© Developmental Studies Center

Grammar and Usage: Recognize and use prepositions and prepositional phrases

Squirrel Skills

A. **Read the passage below. Underline prepositions in one color and prepositional phrases in another.**

Squirrels work hard to keep others away from their food.

A squirrel might dig several holes and only bury a nut in one

of them. It might bury a nut and then pretend to bury another

near the first one. It might bury a nut under a bush, or climb up a

tree and store a nut in a nest, beyond the reach of many animals.

B. **Write a few sentences using at least four of the prepositions below. Underline prepositional phrases in the sentences.**

above	across	against	around
behind	below	beneath	beside
between	beyond	from	in
inside	near	on	outside
over	under		

© Developmental Studies Center

Being a Writer™ | 45

Grammar and Usage: Recognize and divide run-on and very long sentences

Snakes

A. Read the passage below. Divide the run-on sentences.

There are more than two thousand kinds (species) of snakes they come in many sizes the Texas Slender Blind snake is only about five inches long it weighs about 0.1 ounces the Anaconda can grow as long as 33 feet it can weigh up to 550 pounds.

B. Read the very long sentence below. Divide it into shorter sentences. Look for words like *and*, *so*, and *then* to help you divide the sentence.

Many species of snakes kill their prey by wrapping their long body around the animal so they slowly tighten their coils around the victim then once the animal is dead they swallow it whole and they prefer to swallow their prey head first and a snake that squeezes its prey to death is called a constrictor.

46 | Being a Writer™

© Developmental Studies Center

Grammar and Usage: Connect short, related sentences using appositives and participial phrases

Sentence Pairs

A. Turn each sentence into two, short sentences.

Miguel, a bookworm, reads for at least two hours every evening.

Miguel _____

Miguel _____

Stonehenge, a prehistoric monument, was built around 3100 BC.

_____

_____

B. Combine each pair of sentences into a single sentence.

My neighbor is a nurse.

My neighbor works in the emergency ward.

_____

Gorillas are the largest and strongest of the apes.

Gorillas live in Africa.

_____

© Developmental Studies Center

Being a Writer™ | 47

Grammar and Usage: Correctly use commonly misused words

Vacation Daze

A. Read the passage below. Replace the misused words with correct words.

I thought I wood love vacation. I thought it would be grate two have a brake from memorizing facts and righting till my arm drops off. But I never guest I could be so board. I walk buy the creak near our house, counting the ours and days until school starts. I still have another weak too wait. Can you here my groan? I have no patients left! I'm threw with this vacation!

B. Choose any three words from the sets of words below and write a short passage using the words correctly.

to/too/two   there/their/they're

who's/whose   its/it's

your/you're

48 | Being a Writer™   © Developmental Studies Center

Grammar and Usage: Recognize subject-verb agreement with compound subjects

Making Monsters

A. **Read the passage below and underline the verbs.**

My friends and I make papier-mâché monsters. Cara twists wire into shapes. Tod makes the paste. I tear strips of newspaper. Binh puts paste on them and plasters them onto the wire.

B. **Read the passage below with the new people added. Underline the verbs and correct them, if necessary.**

My friends and I make papier-mâché monsters. Cara and Doug twists wire into shapes. Tod and Amy makes the paste. Rob and I tear strips of newspaper. Binh and Leah puts paste on them and plasters them onto the wire.

C. **Read the passage below and correct any incorrect verbs.**

We waits for it to dry. Later, we decorates it. Rob and Tod paints it. Binh glue on eyeballs and antennae. Cara, Doug, and Amy gives advice. I tells silly monster jokes.

© Developmental Studies Center

Being a Writer™ | 49

Grammar and Usage: Recognize and consistently use past, present, and future verb tenses

Refuge or Dump?

A. **Read the passage below. Underline the verbs and mark if they are in past (*pa*), present (*pr*), or future (*f*) tense.**

The Potomac River was once part of a wilderness where a group of Native American tribes lived. After Europeans took over the area, the river became famous for its nearness to our nation's capital, Washington, DC.

Today the river has lots of trash in it. The good news is that every spring, thousands of citizen volunteers clean it up. Young and old alike participate.

What will happen to the Potomac? Maybe people will dump so much garbage in it that cleanup will become difficult. Or maybe they will stop polluting and the river will be trash-free once more.

B. **Write three short paragraphs like those above using past, present, and future verb tenses.**

50 | Being a Writer™   © Developmental Studies Center

Grammar and Usage: Recognize and consistently use first, second, and third person points of view

Life on Mars

A. **Read the passage below. Is it written from the first, second, or third person point of view?**

A finger tapped John's shoulder. He turned over and mumbled sleepily. It was too early to get up! He reached to pat his mother's hand—only to touch cold steel. John bolted upright. He stared at the little robot scurrying out his bedroom door; then he flopped back down on his bed.

Point of view: _____

B. **Rewrite the passage above from a different point of view.**

C. **Write a short passage from the point of view that was not used in step A or B.**

© Developmental Studies Center

Being a Writer™ | 51

Grammar and Usage: Identify and indent paragraphs

Tadpoles

A.   Read the passage below, and then write the main idea of each paragraph.

Tadpoles are the young of toads and frogs. They hatch from eggs and live in the water. If tadpoles can avoid being eaten by other animals, they can mature into adult frogs or toads.

Main idea: _____

A tadpole goes through several stages of growth. After it hatches, it looks like a little black comma with gills. Skin grows over the gills. Legs appear. Lungs grow and the tail shrinks.

Main idea: _____

B.   Insert a paragraph symbol (¶) below wherever a new paragraph should begin.

Tadpoles are fun pets. You can watch as they turn into frogs. You can even play scientist, keeping a notebook and noting observations. Tadpoles are also a responsibility. You need to create a healthy home for them. If you keep them after they've grown, you'll need to create a new habitat for them.

52 | Being a Writer™

© Developmental Studies Center

Grammar and Usage: Recognize and use conjunctions to connect ideas

Get Connected

A.   Read the paragraph below. What do you notice about the underlined words?

Babies have over 100 more bones than adults, <u>so</u> where do those bones go? <u>Since</u> they don't dissolve <u>or</u> evaporate, we must assume they grow together, <u>and</u>, in fact, they do. Many "bones" in a baby's body are made of cartilage. <u>As</u> the baby grows, the material that makes the hard bones of adults replaces the cartilage.

B.   Use some of the following conjunctions to connect ideas in the paragraph below: *and, after, although, as, because, before, but, for, how, however, if, nor, once, or, since, so, than, though, until, when, where, whether, while, yet.*

Your skeleton is light. Your skeleton is strong. To keep it strong, you have to take care of your bones. Being active can strengthen bones. You can dance to be active. You can play sports to be active. Eating foods with calcium also strengthens bones. People think only dairy products have calcium. Sardines, broccoli, tofu, and greens also contain calcium. Taking care of your bones now will help you be a healthy, active adult.

© Developmental Studies Center

Being a Writer™ | 53

Punctuation and Capitalization: Use single and double quotation marks in speech and direct quotation

Great Grandma Remembers

A. **Add single or double quotation marks to the dialogue, as shown below.**

The last time I visited Great Grandma, she described the slang terms she used in the old days.

"We had fun expressions," she explained. "We said 'clam' when we meant 'dollar.'"

Weird, I said. You used a sea animal to describe money.

We used lots of animal words, she said. Instead of saying, I think you're great, we said, You're the cat's pajamas. If we liked something, we said, That's just ducky. We had other fun expressions too. Scram meant leave quickly. I've got the heebie-jeebies meant I'm nervous.

That's just ducky, I said. Great Grandma, you're the cat's pajamas. But I should scram. I promised Dad I'd give him the clam I owe him before 4:00 PM. If I'm late, I'll get the heebie-jeebies!

B. **Write a brief dialogue that includes single and double quotation marks.**

54 | Being a Writer™

© Developmental Studies Center

Punctuation and Capitalization: Use commas in a series

Dark Chocolate, Anyone?

A. **Read the first paragraph below and notice how the commas are used in a series. Then add the missing commas to the second paragraph.**

Do you like chocolate? What kind? Dark chocolate, milk chocolate, or white chocolate? Candy bars, chocolate milk, or hot fudge sauce? Chocolate filled with peanuts, caramel, or cherries? These days (for a price) you can even find chocolate with ingredients like chili peppers, basil, and roses.

Eating too much chocolate can contribute to cavities weight gain and diabetes. But some chocolate may actually be good for you. Dark chocolate has antioxidants. These may help prevent heart disease Alzheimer's disease and cancer. Keep in mind that milk chocolate white chocolate and many chocolate sauces don't have antioxidants. And it's unwise to stuff yourself on *any* sweets— even if they have healing properties!

B. **Write a paragraph using commas in a series.**

© Developmental Studies Center

Being a Writer™ | 55

Punctuation and Capitalization: Capitalize proper nouns including ethnicities, languages, and religions

Almanac Facts

A. **Read the following passage and capitalize letters where needed, as shown below.**

R
͟russia is the world's largest country. It spans 11 time zones and two continents. The country's official language is russian. One of the religions practiced there is russian orthodox.

chile is the world's longest country. It's 2,700 miles long (the same distance as a trip from san francisco to manhattan). It's about twice the size of california. chile's official language is spanish. One religion that chileans practice is roman catholicism.

B. **For each word you capitalized above, write the type of word it is, as shown below.**

- names of languages
- names of religions

C. **Choose two different types of words from the box above. Write five examples for each type, as shown.**

- names of languages: Russian, Spanish, Cantonese, Zulu, Arabic

56 Being a Writer™

© Developmental Studies Center

Punctuation and Capitalization: Cite books and magazine articles

Book Citations

A. Read the book citations below, and then fill in the blanks with the missing information.

Berger, Melvin, and Gilda Berger. *Can It Rain Cats and Dogs? Questions and Answers About Weather.* New York, NY: Scholastic, 1999.

Eubank, Mark. *The Weather Detectives: Fun-Filled Facts, Experiments, and Activities for Kids.* Layton, UT: Gibbs Smith, 2004.

Gibbons, Gail. *Weather Forecasting.* New York, NY: Aladdin, 1993.

A book citation consists of:

Author's last name, _____ .

_____ . _____ ,

_____ : Publisher, _____ .

B. Write three citations using books of your own.

© Developmental Studies Center

Being a Writer™ | **57**

Punctuation and Capitalization: Use parentheses

Sacagawea

A. Read the paragraph below and notice how the parentheses are used.

Sacagawea (Sa-KA-ga-WE-a) was a Native American who traveled with explorers Lewis and Clark through the American Northwest. Along with her husband Touissant Charbonneau (1767–1843) she served as an interpreter. She helped build trust between the explorers (who were white) and the Native American tribes they met. (When tribespeople saw a native woman in the group, they were less suspicious than they might otherwise have been.)

B. Read the paragraph below and add parentheses where appropriate.

Sacagawea whose name means "Bird Woman" was born in 1789 or 1790 the exact year is unknown. Most people believe she died in 1812. Some think she lived until 1884. She was from the Shoshone Sho-SHO-nee tribe. She had two children, Jean Baptiste 1805–1866 and Lisette 1812–?.

C. Write a short passage using parentheses.

58 | Being a Writer™

© Developmental Studies Center

Punctuation and Capitalization: Use colons and semicolons

Camp Is Boring

A. **Read the first letter and notice how colons are used. Insert colons where they belong in the second letter.**

Dear Mom and Dad:

It's 10:00 p.m Tuesday. I've been at camp for two days. Camp

is boring! Please come get me!

Love,

Mollie

Dear Mollie

You only arrived yesterday at 900 a.m. Wait two days; then call

us. If you're still bored, we'll come.

Love,

Mom and Dad

B. **Replace the conjunctions with semicolons in the passage below.**

Mollie called home two days later. "Guess what?" she said.

"Yesterday I saw a bear when we were on a hike. I'm not bored

anymore so don't come get me!"

© Developmental Studies Center

Being a Writer™ | 59

Review: Proofread for grammar, usage, punctuation, and capitalization

The Okapi

A.   Read the passage. Identify and correct the errors.

Have you heard of a creature that looks like a giraffe donkey anteater zebra and antelope? Before the early 1900s, the okapi oh-COP-ee was known only to the natives of the ituri rainforest in africa. Many europeans who herd tails of the animal thought it were a mythical creature like the unicorn. They were proven wrong.

sir harry johnston was a british explorer. Sir Harry Johnston was determined to find the truth about the elusive creature. In 1899 he travels into the Congo wear he heard stories and was shown okapis skulls and skins. In 1901, using Johnstons information, the Zoological Society of London announced the discovery of a new species of forest giraffe. It will be given the scientific name *Okapia Johnstoni.*

B.   Write a passage about something you have learned recently. Proofread it for correctness.

60 | Being a Writer™

© Developmental Studies Center

Student Skill
Practice Book
Corrections

Grammar and Usage: Recognize and use nouns and adjectives

The Smile: Corrections

A. **Nouns are underlined with a solid line and adjectives are underlined with a dotted line. Additional adjectives will vary. Suggestions are shown below.**

grocery
Mr. South works at the store down the road. He has a
....
grumpy
dog named Gerald. Mr. South has angry eyes and
....
a harsh, scratchy voice. Mom says you could scrub an old
....
frying pan with a voice like that.
....

People say that Mr. South doesn't know how to smile.

But when I went to buy bread yesterday, I saw Mr. South
                                                                               ....
patting Gerald. His mouth was curved. His eyes were
                                 ....
little
shining. Then Mr. South saw me. His smile faded. Mom
                                                          ....
wishful
says it was probably all a dream.
                                       ....

B. **Check for the appropriate use of nouns and adjectives in the passage.**

Being a Writer™ | **1**

My Friends: Corrections

A. **Nouns are underlined with a solid line and adjectives are underlined with a dotted line. Additional adjectives will vary. Suggestions are shown below.**

best
My friends are as odd as three socks. Mina has long toes.
....

She used to play the piano with them, but her mom made
                                      ....
her stop.

interesting
Consuela is alert and watchful, like an owl. Consuela
                    ....
imitates every person she meets. So she is also like a talkative
                         ....
parrot.

Chrissy wears a camera around her neck. She wants to
                              ....
become a famous filmmaker. Her latest movie is a thriller.
                    ....
frantic
It's about her mom running late for work.
                 .....

B. **Check for the appropriate use of nouns and adjectives in the passage.**

2 | *Being a Writer™*

---

62 | Being a Writer™ • Grade Four

Grammar and Usage: Recognize and use nouns and adjectives

Locusts: Corrections

A. **Nouns are underlined with a solid line and adjectives are underlined with a dotted line. Additional adjectives will vary. Suggestions are shown below.**

Locusts are large insects. They have big heads, silver wings, and long legs. When they're not flying, they sit in fields of plants, eating everything.

hungry

Locusts usually travel in big swarms. A swarm of locusts is a scary sight. Sometimes, the swarm blocks out the sun, like a storm cloud. The sound of beating wings is loud. Locusts can

dead

turn a field of green plants into a field of bare stalks.

B. **Check for the appropriate use of nouns and adjectives in the passage.**

The African Elephant: Corrections

A. **Nouns are underlined with a solid line and adjectives are underlined with a dotted line. Additional adjectives will vary. Suggestions are shown below.**

The African elephant has gray skin with deep, soft wrinkles. Its forehead is smooth and curved. Its ears are shaped a bit like the continent of Africa. It waves them like

big   annoying

a fan to keep insects away. An elephant uses its trunk like a hand. It can carry an object as heavy as a tree trunk or as

single

small as a blade of grass. An elephant walks with a steady, lumbering stride—but when it's angry or frightened, it can gallop at about 25 miles per hour.

B. **Check for the appropriate use of nouns and adjectives in the passage.**

Being a Writer™ • Grade Four

Grammar and Usage: Recognize and use verbs and adverbs

Whale Watching: Corrections

A. **Verbs are underlined with a solid line and adverbs are underlined with a dotted line. Additional adverbs will vary. Suggestions are shown below.**

On my birthday, Dad and I went sailing. The wind was cold and the sky was dark. Seagulls flew above us, and called

happily

sadly. I wished I was at home, eating ice cream. The sailing trip was Dad's idea.

That was when I saw a smooth, dark shape that curved,

gracefully

out of the sea. I saw a huge tail break the surface of the water. It rose up. Then, slowly, the tail slid back into the water. That creature was as big as an island!

B. **Check for the appropriate use of verbs and adverbs in the passage.**

Being a Writer™ | **5**

---

6 | Being a Writer™

The Trap: Corrections

A. **Verbs are underlined with a solid line and adverbs are underlined with a dotted line. Additional adverbs will vary. Suggestions are shown below.**

The Venus flytrap is a plant that eats flies, spiders, and other bugs. When a fly lands on one of the leaves. The plant

tightly

swings instantly into action. In a second, two leaves clamp,

gradually

shut over the fly. The fly struggles helplessly, but it can't

escape. The plant, eats the fly. Soon, the leaves open again. The plant waits patiently for its next victim.

B. **Check for the appropriate use of verbs and adverbs in the passage.**

64 | Being a Writer™ • Grade Four

Grammar and Usage: Recognize and use verbs and adverbs

The Attic Song: Corrections

A. **Verbs are underlined with a solid line and adverbs are underlined with a dotted line. Additional adverbs will vary. Suggestions are shown below.**

On the weekend, my brother Thom borrowed a drum from school. He carried the drum carefully up the stairs and into the attic. Suddenly, the walls of our house began to shake and quiver. I _cautiously_ looked at Dad. His newspaper shook. Dad muttered gloomily to himself, but I couldn't hear him properly over the noise. I leaped up to get my guitar. I was sure Thom would _eventually_ let me join in. We could start a band in the attic!

B. **Check for the appropriate use of verbs and adverbs in the passage.**

Monster of the Deep: Corrections

A. **Verbs are underlined with a solid line and adverbs are underlined with a dotted line. Additional adverbs will vary. Suggestions are shown below.**

It was November 1861. A boat sailed near the Canary Islands. Suddenly, the crew saw something unusual. They saw long, fleshy arms that trailed through the water. They saw a huge body and eyes as big as dinner plates. The crew _hastily_ panicked. They fired guns. They threw spears. Finally, they tied a rope around the monster's tail. They tried desperately to pull the creature on board. But the creature _smoothly_ slipped into the sea.

B. **Check for the appropriate use of verbs and adverbs in the passage.**

Being a Writer™ • Grade Four

Grammar and Usage: Recognize and use personal and possessive pronouns

---

Whose Lizard? Corrections

A. **Personal pronouns are underlined with a solid line and possessive pronouns are underlined with a dotted line.**

On pet day, people brought their birds, turtles, and rats to school. I brought Allen.

"Whose lizard is this?" Mr. Berry said when he discovered Allen hiding in the curtains. He looked a little scared.

My classmates pointed at me.

B. **Correct pronouns are written in each blank.**

"That's not _____my_____ lizard," _____I_____ said quickly, denying all responsibility.

When I got home, Mom kissed Allen on the head.

_____She_____ loves her lizard.

C. **Check for the appropriate use of pronouns in the passage.**

Being a Writer™ | **9**

Vegetables: Corrections

A. **Personal pronouns are underlined with a solid line and possessive pronouns are underlined with a dotted line.**

Our neighbors have a vegetable garden just like ours.

They have spinach, zucchini, and broccoli, like we have. They have squash, too, but their squash are growing faster than ours.

B. **Correct pronouns are written in each blank.**

"This is terrible!" Mom said, pointing at a squash. "This squash hasn't grown at all."

"None of _____us_____ likes squash, anyway," Dad said to Mom.

"Maybe it feels bad," said Mom. "_____It_____ knows no one likes _____it_____."

C. **Check for the appropriate use of pronouns in the passage.**

10 | *Being a Writer™*

---

66 | *Being a Writer™* • Grade Four

Grammar and Usage: Recognize and use personal and possessive pronouns

In the Morning: Corrections

A. **Personal pronouns are underlined with a solid line and possessive pronouns are underlined with a dotted line.**

Dad came storming into the bedroom. "Whose is this?"

he demanded, holding up a wet towel.

AJ and I looked at each other. "Not mine," we both said.

"Somebody left it on the bathroom floor," said Dad.

B. **Correct pronouns are written in each blank.**

"It must be ___yours___," I told AJ. "I haven't had

___my___ shower yet."

AJ frowned at me. "I haven't had ___mine___ either!" he said.

Dad stared at ___us___. "Maybe it was the cat," he

said wearily.

C. **Check for the appropriate use of pronouns in the passage.**

Being a Writer™ | **11**

Pancakes: Corrections

A. **Personal pronouns are underlined with a solid line and possessive pronouns are underlined with a dotted line.**

Yesterday, Astrid and I made pancakes. For some reason,

my pancakes turned out better than Astrid's pancakes. When

all the pancakes were ready, she took the ones I had made! I

was left with her lumpy ones.

B. **Correct pronouns are written in each blank.**

"Hey," I said, "you didn't make ___those___."

"It doesn't matter," Astrid said. "___They___ will all

taste the same."

"But…the pancakes on your plate are ___mine___," I said.

"Not any more," Astrid said as she squirted maple syrup

all over ___them___.

C. **Check for the appropriate use of pronouns in the passage.**

12 | *Being a Writer™*

Being a Writer™ • Grade Four | **67**

Grammar and Usage: Recognize and use personal pronouns, possessive pronouns, and possessive adjectives

Whose Lizard? Corrections

A. Personal pronouns are underlined with a solid line and possessive adjectives are underlined with a double line.

On pet day, people brought their birds, turtles, and rats to school. I brought Allen.

"Whose lizard is this?" Mr. Berry said when he discovered Allen hiding in the curtains. He looked a little scared.

My classmates pointed at me.

B. Correct words are written in each blank.

"That's not ___*my*___ lizard," ___*I*___ said quickly, denying all responsibility.

When I got home, Mom kissed Allen on the head.

C. Check for the appropriate use of possessive adjectives in the passage.

___*She*___ loves her lizard.

Being a Writer™ | **9**

Vegetables: Corrections

A. Personal pronouns are underlined with a solid line, possessive pronouns are underlined with a dotted line, and possessive adjectives are underlined with a double line.

Our neighbors have a vegetable garden just like ours.

They have spinach, zucchini, and broccoli, like we have.

They have squash, too, but their squash are growing faster than ours.

B. Correct words are written in each blank.

"This is terrible!" Mom said, pointing at a squash. "This squash hasn't grown at all."

"None of ___*us*___ likes squash, anyway," Dad said to Mom.

"Maybe it feels bad," said Mom. " ___*It*___ knows no one likes ___*it*___ ."

C. Check for the appropriate use of possessive adjectives in the passage.

10 | *Being a Writer*™

66 | Being a Writer™ • Grade Four

Grammar and Usage: Recognize and use personal pronouns, possessive pronouns, and possessive adjectives

In the Morning: Corrections

A. **Personal pronouns are underlined with a solid line and possessive pronouns are underlined with a dotted line.**

Dad came storming into the bedroom. "Whose is this?"

he demanded, holding up a wet towel.

AJ and I looked at each other. "Not mine," we both said.

"Somebody left it on the bathroom floor," said Dad.

B. **Correct words are written in each blank.**

"It must be ___yours___," I told AJ. "I haven't had

___my___ shower yet."

AJ frowned at me. "I haven't had ___mine___ either!" he said.

Dad stared at ___us___. "Maybe it was the cat," he

said wearily.

C. **Check for the appropriate use of possessive adjectives in the passage.**

Being a Writer™ | 11

Pancakes: Corrections

A. **Personal pronouns are underlined with a solid line and possessive adjectives are underlined with a double line.**

Yesterday, Astrid and I made pancakes. For some reason,

my pancakes turned out better than Astrid's pancakes. When

all the pancakes were ready, she took the ones I had made! I

was left with her lumpy ones.

B. **Correct words are written in each blank.**

"Hey," I said, "you didn't make ___those___!"

"It doesn't matter," Astrid said. "___They___ will all

taste the same."

"But...the pancakes on your plate are ___mine___," I said.

"Not anymore," Astrid said as she squirted maple syrup

all over ___them___.

C. **Check for the appropriate use of possessive adjectives in the passage.**

12 | Being a Writer™

Being a Writer™ • Grade Four | 67

Grammar and Usage: Recognize and divide run-on and very long sentences

Up the Hill: Corrections

A. Corrections appear below.

The worst part of my bike ride home from school is the last bend. That's where the road climbs a steep hill. I push my feet against the pedals and begin to climb. My muscles start to burn and my shoulders begin to ache. Sweat gathers inside my helmet and drips into my eyes. I pedal and pedal until my lungs are about to explode. I must be near the top by now but I can't slow down. I just have to keep going inch by inch until I get there.

B. Corrections appear below.

My mom and sister and I live at the top of the steepest hill in town. And when you're biking up the hill, it looks as though our house is right on the edge of the world. Then when you get there, you see that the world just keeps going all the way past our house. So my sister says we're lucky to live where we do because if there's a big flood we will be safe. And I suppose she has a point.

17

Being a Writer™

Mighty Mold: Corrections

A. Corrections appear below.

Mold grows on things like bread. It is white. It looks soft and furry. Hopefully, you won't discover the mold when you are eating a sandwich. Hopefully, you will discover it before you take the first bite.

B. Corrections appear below.

One of the world's most important medicines comes from mold. And it is called penicillin. And it was discovered by a man named Alexander Fleming. Then Fleming left a dish of germs near a window and mold grew in the dish. Fleming was about to throw the dish away. But then he looked closely. He saw that the mold had eaten the germs.

18

Being a Writer™

70 | Being a Writer™ • Grade Four

Grammar and Usage: Recognize and divide run-on and very long sentences

---

Coffee: Corrections

A. Corrections appear below.

My older brother loves coffee. I wanted to know why he likes it so much, so the other day he brewed some fresh coffee and poured me a cup. It smelled really good. I took a huge gulp. It tasted like melted tar. I managed to swallow it but it took three days to get the taste out of my mouth.

I can't believe my brother drinks that stuff.

B. Corrections appear below.

My brother says that your tastes change as you get older. He says that coffee could end up being my favorite drink, but I don't believe him. Ever since he went to college, he pretends to know everything. All that coffee must be affecting his brain. and *something* is, anyway.

No Water: Corrections

A. Corrections appear below.

A drought is when there is no rain for a long time. In a drought the water in rivers and wells dries up. Farm animals suffer and plants die. Fires erupt easily in forests and they spread quickly. Deep cracks form in the ground as though the earth is gasping for water. People must use every drop of water carefully and hope that rain will fall.

B. Corrections appear below.

It's difficult to know when a drought will happen. However scientists have found that dry times often follow rainy times. And they can trace dry times and rainy times by looking at how fast trees have grown. Because in rainy years trees grow fast. And in dry years trees grow slower.

Being a Writer™ • Grade Four | 71

Grammar and Usage: Connect short, related sentences using appositives and participial phrases

---

Sentence Pairs: Corrections

A. Corrections are shown below.

My best friend, a soccer player, taught me how to play soccer.

My best friend _is a soccer player._

My best friend _taught me how to play soccer._

Poodles, a breed of dog, are favorite family pets.

Poodles are a breed of dog.

Poodles are favorite family pets.

B. Corrections are shown below.

Feelings are normal.

Feelings can help you make decisions.

Feelings, which are normal, can help you make decisions.

My parents are waving.

My parents are standing in the back row.

My parents are standing in the back row, waving.

Being a Writer™ | **21**

Sentence Pairs: Corrections

A. Corrections are shown below.

My teacher, a native Chinese speaker, taught me how to speak Chinese.

My teacher _is a native Chinese speaker._

My teacher _taught me how to speak Chinese._

Tae Kwon Do, a Korean martial art, requires focus and discipline.

Tae Kwon Do is a Korean martial art.

Tae Kwon Do requires strong focus and discipline.

B. Corrections are shown below.

The mountain is too dangerous to climb.

The mountain is cold and steep.

The mountain, cold and steep, is too dangerous to climb.

The dog is barking loudly.

The dog is driving me mad.

The dog barking loudly is driving me mad.

22 | Being a Writer™

72 | Being a Writer™ • Grade Four

Grammar and Usage: Connect short, related sentences using appositives and participial phrases

Sentence Pairs: Corrections

A. Corrections are shown below.

My cousin, a juggler, knows how to juggle eight oranges.

My cousin _is a juggler._

My cousin _knows how to juggle eight oranges._

My favorite T-shirt, the one with the holes, needs to be washed.

My favorite T-shirt is the one with the holes.

My favorite T-shirt needs to be washed.

B. Corrections are shown below.

The baby is making a lot of noise.

The baby is not my sister.

The baby making a lot of noise is not my sister.

My favorite food is fresh bread.

My favorite food is easy to make when you know how.

My favorite food, fresh bread, is easy to make when you know how.

Sentence Pairs: Corrections

A. Corrections are shown below.

My aunt, a carpenter, builds her own furniture.

My aunt _is a carpenter._

My aunt _builds her own furniture._

My favorite flavor, chocolate, is everyone else's favorite, too.

My favorite flavor is chocolate.

My favorite flavor is everyone else's favorite, too.

B. Corrections are shown below.

My grandmother is a great piano player.

My grandmother taught me how to read music.

My grandmother, a great piano player, taught me how to read music.

The boy is playing the guitar.

The boy is my brother.

The boy playing the guitar is my brother.

Being a Writer™ • Grade Four | 73

Grammar and Usage: Correctly use commonly misused words

The Pear Tree: Corrections

A. Corrections are shown below.

There
~~Their~~ is a pear tree across the fence. It is a monster of
pear
a ~~pair~~ tree. It must be thirty feet high! The problem is that
whose
my neighbors and I can't agree ~~who's~~ tree it is.
It's
"~~Its~~ my tree," says my neighbor, "because ~~its~~ growing on
It's
my side of the fence."

I think the tree belongs to me because it leans over the
sit
fence. I like to ~~set~~ down underneath the tree. I stretch out
lie
and ~~lay~~ in the shade, surrounded by the ~~cent~~ of ~~pairs~~.
scent *pears*

B. Check for the correct use of commonly misused words in the passage.

Running Away: Corrections

A. Corrections are shown below.

On the morning we ran away from home, Sonia and I
rise
climbed a hill. We watched the sun ~~raise~~.

"What should we do today?" Sonia asked.

sales
"We could visit the mall," I said. "We could check out
the clothing ~~sails~~!"

except
"~~accept~~ people will see us and tell our parents that we've
run away."

Sonia raised her eyebrows. "Great idea," she said,

hours
We had been on the run for only a few ~~ours~~, and I
already
missed home ~~all ready~~.

B. Check for the correct use of commonly misused words in the passage.

Grammar and Usage: Correctly use commonly misused words

Earth's Fireworks: Corrections

A. **Corrections are shown below.**

A volcano is like a fireworks display put on by Earth.

Huge clouds of fire shoot out of the mountain. Rivers of

burning rock slide down ~~it's~~ *its* sides. Hot ash pours out of the

mountaintop and chunks of rock are ~~throne~~ *thrown* high into the

air. If the volcano is strong enough, it could blow the ~~hole~~ *whole*

mountain to pieces.

B. **Check for the correct use of commonly misused words in the passage.**

Frida Kahlo: Corrections

A. **Corrections appear in bold.**

Frida Kahlo was a Mexican artist. She wanted ~~too~~ *to*

become a doctor. But when she was fifteen, she was hurt in

a terrible bus crash. She wasn't able ~~too~~ *to* study medicine, so

she taught herself ~~two~~ *to* paint. She didn't paint exactly what

she saw. Instead, she painted things she imagined. In one

painting, ~~their~~ *there* are ~~too~~ *two* Fridas sitting together.

B. **Check for the correct use of commonly misused words in the passage.**

Being a Writer™ • Grade Four

Grammar and Usage: Recognize subject-verb agreement with compound subjects

The Artists: Corrections

A. **Verbs are underlined below.**

On Sunday mornings, my brother Jake spreads newspaper over the dining table and paints. My sister Winona scribbles poems in her notebook. I cut pictures out of magazines and arrange them on my bedroom wall. Dad switches on the stereo and dances around the kitchen. He sings loudly as he makes lunch.

B. **All verbs are underlined, and necessary corrections to verbs are shown below.**

On Sunday mornings, my mom and my brother Jake
spread
~~spreads~~ newspaper over the dining table and paints. My
paint
sister Winona and her friend Nelly ~~scribbles~~ poems in
scribble
their notebooks. My friend Ramona and I cut pictures out
of magazines and arrange them on my bedroom wall. Dad
switch
and Grandma ~~switches~~ on the stereo and ~~dances~~ around the
dance
sing   *make*
kitchen. They ~~sings~~ loudly as they ~~makes~~ lunch.

On the Weekend: Corrections

A. **Verbs are underlined below.**

On the weekend, Sam travels up the Amazon River. Unfortunately, he forgets insect repellent. As mosquitoes eat him alive, Sam abandons his boat and swims up the river instead. Some stingrays, pink dolphins, piranhas, and crocodiles keep him company as he swims.

B. **All verbs are underlined, and necessary corrections to verbs are shown below.**

travel
On the weekend, Sam and his friend Kat ~~travels~~ up the
Forget
Amazon River. Unfortunately, they ~~forgets~~ insect repellent.
abandon
As mosquitoes eat them alive, Sam and Kat ~~abandons~~ their
swim
boat and ~~swims~~ up the river instead. Some stingrays, pink
dolphins, piranhas, and crocodiles keep them company as
swim
they ~~swims~~.

Grammar and Usage: Recognize subject-verb agreement with compound subjects

---

Camping with Lionel: Corrections

A.   Verbs are underlined below.

On the first day, it rains. There are leaks in our cabin.

My friend Lionel dashes around. He puts salad bowls under

all the leaks. Lionel's sister Joanne covers the furniture with

sheets. I do, too. Mrs. Darby stands on a chair and seals the

leaks with sticky tape.

B.   All verbs are underlined, and necessary corrections to verbs are shown below.

On the first day, it rains. There are leaks in our cabin.

                                 dash   *put*

My friend Lionel and I ~~dashes~~ around. We ~~puts~~ salad bowls

                                                     cover

under all the leaks. Lionel's sisters Joanne and Chelsea ~~covers~~

                                                                                                                                                                                                    stand   *seal*

the furniture with sheets. I do, too. Mr. and Mrs. Darby ~~stands~~ on chairs and ~~seals~~ the leaks with sticky tape.

All That Jazz: Corrections

A.   Verbs are underlined below.

You hear many different sounds when you listen to a

band. A drummer plays the rhythm. Three saxophones play

the song. A clarinet climbs up and down the scale. The

players' fingers move very fast.

B.   All verbs are underlined, and necessary corrections to verbs are shown below.

You hear many different sounds when you listen to a

                                           play

band. A drummer and a percussionist ~~plays~~ the rhythm.

                                                      play

Three saxophones and a trombone ~~plays~~ the song. A clarinet

                             climb

and a flute ~~climbs~~ up and down the scale. The players'

fingers move very fast.

Grammar and Usage: Recognize and consistently use past, present, and future verb tenses

---

Who Is Louis Sachar? Corrections

A. Verbs are underlined and marked to signify past (pa), present (pr), and future (f) tense.

Louis Sachar was [pa] born in New York in 1954. When he was [pa] nine, his family moved [pa] to California. Orange trees grew [pa] all around. Louis and his friends had [pa] fights with the mushy, rotten fruit underneath the trees.

Today, Louis Sachar dreams [pr] up crazy ideas for children's books. He says [pr] that it is [pr] a thrill to start [pr] with a blank page and finish with a whole story. Louis keeps [pr] his stories secret until he writes [pr] the very last word.

Louis might write [f] a book for adults one day. His adult characters probably won't have the same kinds of adventures as his young characters, but hopefully, the stories will be [f] just as action-packed.

B. Check for the appropriate use of verb tense in the paragraphs.

Summers: Corrections

A. Verbs are underlined and marked to signify past (pa), present (pr), and future (f) tense.

Years ago, my family and I spent [pa] summers at Granddad's place. Dad usually disappeared [pa] into the woods with his *Field Guide for Birds* book. Mom collected [pa] plants. I hung [pa] out in the barn with my big brother as he took [pa] Granddad's old cars to pieces.

Now that my brother is [pr] gone, we go [pr] to the lake. Mom and Dad lie [pr] on the sand and swat [pr] sandflies. I swim [pr]. Everything is [pr] boring without my brother.

One day, I will leave [f] home and my parents will go [f] on great holidays again. They will sigh [f] with relief. "Finally, we will go [f] somewhere really amazing." Mom will say [f].

B. Check for the appropriate use of verb tense in the paragraphs.

Grammar and Usage: Recognize and consistently use past, present, and future verb tenses

How Will We Travel? Corrections

A. Verbs are underlined and marked to signify past (*pa*), present (*pr*), and future (*f*) tense.

Long, long ago, people traveled [pa] only on foot. They hoisted [pa] loads onto their backs, balanced [pa] them on their heads, or dragged [pa] them along the ground. About 5000 BC, people strapped [pa] loads to the backs of animals.

Today, on a jet airliner, travelers move [pr] as fast as the speed of sound. Trains, trucks, and cargo ships haul [pr] goods all over the globe. Millions of people watch [pr] the world flash [pr] by from inside cars, buses, and trains.

In the future, maybe the trains will hover [f] above the ground. Maybe cars will drive [f] themselves. Perhaps no one will walk [f] anymore.

B. Check for the appropriate use of verb tense in the paragraphs.

Being a Writer™ | **35**

Fearless: Corrections

A. Verbs are underlined and marked to signify past (*pa*), present (*pr*), and future (*f*) tense.

Once, I was [pa] frightened of the dark. I thought [pa] that the dark swallowed [pa] people who closed [pa] their eyes. So my dad bought [pa] me a night lamp. It glowed [pa] beside my bed. Somehow, it helped [pa] me see that the dark was [pa] not as scary as it looked [pa].

I am [pr] not afraid of the dark anymore, but now I feel [pr] nervous about the future. I worry [pr] about many things. People think [pr] I am [pr] fearless, but that is [pr] not true.

Perhaps one day, I will overcome [f] my fears. Perhaps they will fade [f] and will become [f] nothing more than shadows.

B. Check for the appropriate use of verb tense in the paragraphs.

36 | *Being a Writer™*

Being a Writer™ • Grade Four | **79**

Grammar and Usage: Recognize and consistently use first, second, and third person points of view

Summer Camp: Corrections

A.   The first passage is written from the second person point of view.

B.   Check that the passage is rewritten from the first or third person point of view.

C.   Check the passage for consistent point of view.

Dreams: Corrections

A.   The first passage is written from the third person point of view.

B.   Check that the passage is rewritten from the first or second person point of view.

C.   Check the passage for consistent point of view.

Grammar and Usage: Recognize and consistently use first, second, and third person points of view

George: Corrections

A. The first passage is written from the first person point of view.

B. Check that the passage is rewritten from the second or third person point of view.

C. Check the passage for consistent point of view.

The Three-Legged Race: Corrections

A. The first passage is written from the third person point of view.

B. Check that the passage is rewritten from the first or second person point of view.

C. Check the passage for consistent point of view.

Being a Writer™ • Grade Four | 81

Grammar and Usage: Identify and indent paragraphs

Route 66: Corrections

A. The main idea of each paragraph is given below.

U.S. Route 66 is a famous highway in America. It opened in 1926. It linked Chicago and Los Angeles. Some people called it the "Main Street of America." If you lived in a small town, Route 66 was your link to a big city.

Main idea: *Route 66 is a famous American highway.*

In the 1950s, people began building freeways so that they could travel faster. Slowly, parts of Route 66 were replaced with freeways. Route 66 was never the same.

Main idea: *Route 66 changed because people needed better roads.*

B. The paragraph symbol (¶) is shown where it makes sense to begin a new paragraph.

¶
People still like to travel on old Route 66. They eat in old diners and stay in roadside motels. They visit museums and other sights along the way. ¶ Today, there are companies that take people on tours of Route 66. You can even take a tour by motorcycle!

Being a Writer™ | **41**

Big Bad Wolves: Corrections

A. The main idea of each paragraph is given below.

Many people are afraid of wolves. Wolves are dangerous in many stories. In "Little Red Riding Hood," a wolf threatens to eat a little girl. In "The Three Little Pigs," a wolf bullies three helpless pigs.

Main idea: *Wolves are shy animals.*

The truth is, wolves are very shy. They live in places where there are not a lot of people. They usually run when they see or smell people.

Main idea: *Most people are afraid of wolves.*

B. The paragraph symbol (¶) is shown where it makes sense to begin a new paragraph.

¶
People's fear of wolves has led them to kill them. In the past, the U.S. government encouraged people to kill wolves. ¶ Sadly, so many wolves have been killed that some kinds are in danger of disappearing forever. For example, the red wolf and the grey wolf are nearly extinct in the U.S.

82 | Being a Writer™ • Grade Four

Grammar and Usage: Identify and indent paragraphs

My Brother Tristan: Corrections

A. **The main idea of each paragraph is given below.**

My brother Tristan and I fight a lot. He is very stubborn. He's also funny and smart, but I forget that when we fight. So far, I think we have had about a million fights.

Main idea: *My brother Tristan and I fight a lot.*

Yesterday we had a fight over raspberry jello. Tristan finished his jello and wanted mine. When I said "No," he stuck his chubby hand right into my bowl! I was mad!

Main idea: *Yesterday we had a fight about jello.*

B. **The paragraph symbol (¶) is shown where it makes sense to begin a new paragraph.**

¶ For a long time, Tristan and I fought over objects. We fought about toys. We fought about books. We fought about food. Now, our fights are different. For example, yesterday ¶ we had a fight about which kind of dog we like. Our fights are more like talking now, but with more shouting.

Desert Life: Corrections

A. **The main idea of each paragraph is given below.**

In the desert, the only place with water is an oasis. An oasis is a place in the desert with a spring. In large deserts, like the Sahara, people build towns near oases.

Main idea: *An oasis is the only place with water in the desert.*

Desert animals use oases, too. Gazelles, antelope, snakes, and small foxes get water from the oasis. They also eat the plants that grow there.

Main idea: *Animals use oases too.*

B. **The paragraph symbol (¶) is shown where it makes sense to begin a new paragraph.**

¶ If you visited the Sahara Desert ten thousand years ago, you would not know it was a desert. Back then, the Sahara had lakes, streams, grass, and trees. People and animals lived ¶ there. But, about six thousand years ago, the Sahara became hotter and drier. Eventually, the Sahara became so dry that very few people or animals lived there anymore.

Being a Writer™ • Grade Four | 83

Grammar and Usage: Recognize and use conjunctions to connect ideas

Dragons: Corrections

A. **The underlined words in the paragraph below are all conjunctions, or words that connect or show relationships among ideas.**

A dragon is an imaginary animal that many cultures have stories about. While many European stories show dragons as frightening and ugly, many Asian stories show dragons as neither frightening nor ugly. Instead, they represent good luck!

B. **Examples of ways to use conjunctions in the paragraph are given below.**

In China, people are building a giant dragon sculpture. It will curve along the ridge of a mountain. The dragon's head will be 100 feet high. Its body will be 30 feet high. Its
       and it's
body will be 20 feet wide. It will be covered in nearly six
    and
million pieces of marble and bronze. These pieces will form
scales. The scales will represent the many different cultures
  that
of China.

Being a Writer™ | **45**

The Bicycle Club: Corrections

A. **The underlined words in the paragraph below are all conjunctions, or words that connect or show relationships among ideas.**

If you want to join my bicycle club, your bicycle must have a name. Bike or Cycle is not a good name. However, a name like Torpedo or Meteor would be better, although the name should always mean something to you personally.

B. **Examples of ways to use conjunctions in the paragraph are given below.**

       because
I started a bicycle club. I've always thought that bicycles are wonderful. They'll take you almost anywhere you want to go. Did you know that there are about one billion bicycles in the world? That is more than twice the number of cars. It's much more exciting to ride a bicycle than to ride in a car-
  because you
You experience the journey more!

46 | *Being a Writer™*

84 | Being a Writer™ • Grade Four

Grammar and Usage: Recognize and use conjunctions to connect ideas

---

Inventions: Corrections

A. **The underlined words in the paragraph below are all conjunctions, or words that connect or show relationships among ideas.**

Experiments can be exciting, but they can also lead

to unexpected results. I know this because I do lots of

experiments as an inventor. I am working on an invention

that will make people taller. Since I have not invented it yet,

I can't tell you how it will work.

B. **Examples of ways to use conjunctions in the paragraph are given below.**

Ideas for inventions are all around. It's simply a matter

of looking for ways to make things better. ~~Imagine that~~ *When*

something annoys you, imagine how you might solve the

problem. ~~You might~~ *If you* get annoyed when you lose your socks~~.~~ *, you*

~~You~~ could invent flashing lights to go on your socks~~. Now~~ *so*

they'll be easy to find.

48 | Being a Writer™

Making Music: Corrections

A. **The underlined words in the paragraph below are all conjunctions, or words that connect or show relationships among ideas.**

Before you decide which musical instrument you'd like

to play, do some research. Although instruments like the

saxophone are fun, there are lots of cool instruments out

there. You may have tried the trumpet, but have you tried a

trombone? Once you've learned how to play the piano, you

should try the electric keyboard.

B. **Examples of ways to use conjunctions in the paragraph are given below.**

The Treholipee is an odd-looking musical instrument~~. It~~ *that*

, but you was popular for a very short time~~. It~~

~~You~~ won't see many of them around today. Its body looks like a

small guitar~~. Its~~ *and its* neck is long and curved.

Being a Writer™ | 47

Being a Writer™ • Grade Four | 85

Punctuation and Capitalization: Use single and double quotation marks in speech and direct quotation

Sun and Storm: Corrections

A. Correct use of single and double quotation marks is shown below.

My aunt Jen used to live in Japan. One of her favorite Japanese stories is the one about the sun.

"Once, there was a girl named Sun," Aunt Jen tells my brother and me. "She was so dazzling that her parents said, 'Why don't we put her in the sky?'"

Then Aunt Jen tells how Sun went to live in the sky where she gave warmth and light to plants and animals on Earth. She was a total superstar. But Sun also had a brother named Storm.

"Storm was a control freak," Aunt Jen explains. "He liked being in charge. He stomped around making valleys with his feet and tearing up trees with his breath."

"He sounds like you," I tell my brother.

B. Check for the appropriate use of single and double quotation marks in the dialogue.

Being a Writer™ **49**

Not-so-scary Stories: Corrections

A. Correct use of single and double quotation marks is shown below.

When I was small, my mom would try to tell me scary stories. She would sit beside my bed, holding a flashlight under her chin to make her look like a ghost.

"It was a dark and stormy night," Mom said. "A boy named Elroy couldn't sleep."

"Why not?" I asked.

"Because the wind was making a strange sound outside his window," Mom said. "It sounded as though it was saying, 'El-roy... El-roy...'"

"I don't like this story," I said.

"Wait until you hear what happens," said Mom. "Elroy got up and went to the window. He heard the wind say, 'Hey, Elroy! It's cold out. Let me in.'"

"This is not a scary story," I said.

B. Check for the appropriate use of single and double quotation marks in the dialogue.

50 | *Being a Writer™*

86 | Being a Writer™ • Grade Four

Punctuation and Capitalization: Use single and double quotation marks in speech and direct quotation

Eileen: Corrections

A. **Correct use of single and double quotation marks is shown below.**

My friend Dave has a baby sister named Eileen. She makes noises, but doesn't talk yet. Dave is pretty good at figuring out what she's saying.

"When she yells, it means she's tired, but it can mean other stuff, too," Dave explained to me. "One time, it meant, 'Hey, Dave, let's build a spaceship.' So we built this awesome spaceship in the living room."

Just then, Eileen started howling. Dave's mom picked her up and said, "This one's easy. She's saying, 'Feed me.'"

"No, she's not," Dave said. "She's saying, 'I'm bored. Let's go to the movies.'"

Dave's mom frowned. "How do you know?"

"I just know," Dave said.

B. **Check for the appropriate use of single and double quotation marks in the dialogue.**

Being a Writer™ | **51**

Waldo the Great: Corrections

A. **Correct use of single and double quotation marks is shown below.**

Yesterday, I helped my neighbor Mr. Kite take his dog Waldo for a walk. We were about to cross a bridge when Waldo came to a stop.

"Oh no! He always does this," Mr. Kite groaned.

I bent down and said, "What's up, Waldo? Is there a bad smell around here?"

Waldo woofed softly and showed the whites of his eyes.

"Maybe he's saying, 'My legs are sore,'" I told Mr. Kite.

Mr. Kite shook his head. "I know what the problem is," he said. "Waldo is saying, 'I can't stand heights, water, or fish, and I won't cross the bridge unless somebody carries me.'"

I sighed and said, "OK." I picked up Waldo and tucked him under my arm.

B. **Check for the appropriate use of single and double quotation marks in the dialogue.**

52 | Being a Writer™

Being a Writer™ • Grade Four | 87

Punctuation and Capitalization: Use commas in a series

Spring: Corrections

A. **Correct use of commas in the second paragraph of the passage is shown below.**

Then I wash the curtains, wipe down the walls, and stand on a ladder to mop the ceiling. I rescue all the spiders, caterpillars, and cockroaches and put them in the garden. I dust every leaf of my indoor plants. I have five angel ivy trees, twenty ponytail palm trees, and six Chinese evergreen trees. Finally, I wash the dog, the cat, and the gerbil. Everything is clean!

B. **Check for the appropriate use of commas in a series in the sentences.**

How to Name a Pet: Corrections

A. **Correct use of commas in the second paragraph of the passage is shown below.**

I think the best way to name your pet is to look at it carefully. My dog has black fur. I thought about naming him Shadow, Smokey, or Bandit. He loves to run. I thought of Runner, Speed, and Jumper. Finally, I decided on Buster. I think he looks like a Buster.

B. **Check for the appropriate use of commas in a series in the sentences.**

Punctuation and Capitalization: Use commas in a series

Mohammed's Story: Corrections

A. Correct use of commas in the second paragraph of the passage is shown below.

My life is so different now! Everything I see, hear, touch, and taste is new. I've learned new words, new sports, and new ideas. I've eaten new foods, like waffles, bagels, and granola. I've found new friends, new traditions, and a new home.

B. Check for the appropriate use of commas in a series in the sentences.

Picnic Ingredients: Corrections

A. Correct use of commas in the second paragraph of the passage is shown below.

Let's say it's a sunny day. Pack some food into a bag, basket, or box. Sandwiches, salads, cakes, and cookies are all excellent. Don't forget something to drink. If you plan to walk through a park, climb a hill, or go exploring, you'll get thirsty. Other things to take include a map, a camera, and a few friends.

B. Check for the appropriate use of commas in a series in the sentences.

Being a Writer™ • Grade Four

Punctuation and Capitalization: Capitalize proper nouns including ethnicities, languages, and religions

New Year's in Thailand: Corrections

A. Corrections are shown below.

In t͟hailand, the new year starts in a͟pril. It is a time
of cleaning and new life. One tradition is to throw water.
People use hoses and water pistols to drench one another.
People carry b͟uddhist statues through the streets so that
passersby can splash them with water.

B. Types of proper nouns in the passage are shown below.

- *names of countries*
- *names of religions*
- *months of the year*
- *names of cities*
- *ethnicities or nationalities*
- *names of special events*

C. Check for appropriate examples of the selected types of proper nouns.

Japanese New Year's: Corrections

A. Corrections are shown below.

j͟apanese people celebrate the new year on january 1.
The celebration is similar to c͟hristmas. People send one
another cards, sing songs, and eat lots of food. j͟apanese
children are given money in a tradition called "o͟toshidama"
that came from c͟hina. On n͟ew y͟ear's d͟ay, people celebrate
the first things of the year. They watch the first sunrise and
celebrate the first smile they see.

B. Types of proper nouns in the passage are shown below.

- *names of ethnicities or nationalities*
- *names of languages*
- *names of special events*
- *names of countries*

C. Check for appropriate examples of the selected types of proper nouns.

Punctuation and Capitalization: Capitalize proper nouns including ethnicities, languages, and religions

Rosh Hashanah: Corrections

A. Corrections are shown below.

Rosh hashanah is the jewish new year celebration.

The Hebrew words "rosh hashanah" mean "beginning of

the year," though the holiday usually begins in september.

When it begins, people blow a trumpet made from a ram's

horn to alert people that the year has begun. Otherwise,

Rosh hashanah is a very quiet holiday. People say prayers,

recite poetry, and eat traditional foods like apples and honey.

B. Types of proper nouns in the passage are shown below.

- names of holidays
- names of languages
- names of states
- ethnicities or nationalities
- months of the year

C. Check for appropriate examples of the selected types of proper nouns.

Spanish: Corrections

A. Corrections are shown below.

Spanish is the second most common language in

the united states after english. In 2000, there were

28.1 million people in the U.S. who spoke spanish most

frequently at home. About half of all spanish speakers

also spoke english fluently.

B. Types of proper nouns in the passage are shown below.

- names of languages
- names of countries

C. Check for appropriate examples of the selected types of proper nouns.

Being a Writer™ • Grade Four 91

Punctuation and Capitalization: Cite books and magazine articles

Book Citations: Corrections

A. The completed model for book citations is shown below.

Author's last name , Author's first name.

Book title in italics . City where published, State:

Publisher ; Copyright year .

B. Check for the correct order of information and the correct use of punctuation and capitalization in the citations.

Book Citations: Corrections

A. The completed model for book citations is shown below.

Author's last name, *Author's first name* .

Book title in italics . City where published

State : Publisher, Copyright year .

B. Check for the correct order of information and the correct use of punctuation and capitalization in the citations.

Punctuation and Capitalization: Cite books and magazine articles

---

Magazine Article Citations: Corrections

A. The completed model for magazine article citations is shown below.

Author's last name, ___Author's First name___.

" ___Title of article___." ___Title of magazine in italics___,

Month and year article was published: ___Page numbers___.

B. Check for the correct order of information and the correct use of punctuation and capitalization in the citations.

Being a Writer™ | **63**

Magazine Article Citations: Corrections

A. The completed model for magazine article citations is shown below.

___Author's last name___, ___Author's First name___.

"Title of article." *Title of magazine in italics,*

___Month and year when published___ : Page numbers.

B. Check for the correct order of information and the correct use of punctuation and capitalization in the citations.

64 | *Being a Writer™*

Being a Writer™ • Grade Four | 93

Punctuation and Capitalization: Use parentheses

Wild Stories: Corrections

B. Correct use of parentheses in the second paragraph of the passage is shown below.

Some say that Calamity Jane once swam (90 miles 145 kilometers) up the Platte River. Others tell stories of how she was thrown out of many towns (usually for shooting up the saloon). One story has it that Calamity Jane pulled two guns on some cowboys in a saloon in North Dakota (she aimed at their feet and told them to dance for their lives).

C. Check for the appropriate use of parentheses in the passage.

The Library: Corrections

B. Correct use of parentheses in the second paragraph of the passage is shown below.

If there is any sound Mr. Ernest likes less than talking, it's laughing (he doesn't like singing much, either). As you know, laughter is contagious (it spreads like the flu). Once I start laughing, I get all my friends laughing (and in trouble too).

C. Check for the appropriate use of parentheses in the passage.

Punctuation and Capitalization: Use parentheses

Paul Bunyan, Man of Mystery: Corrections

B. Correct use of parentheses in the second paragraph of the passage is shown below.

In the early 1900s, James MacGillivray (a young newspaper reporter) told the first stories about Paul Bunyan. Some of these stories included other characters, like Dutch Jake (another lumberjack) and Sailor Jake (Paul Bunyan's enemy). Today, there are statues of Paul Bunyan all over America. One is in Oscoda, Michigan (said to be his first home).

C. Check for the appropriate use of parentheses in the passage.

The Painter: Corrections

B. Correct use of parentheses in the second paragraph of the passage is shown below.

Every day, when I get home from school, I see Henry painting in his yard. He always paints outdoors (his favorite painter also painted outdoor). Henry's cat is named Vincent (after Vincent Van Gogh). Henry isn't a famous painter (but he seems very happy).

C. Check for the appropriate use of parentheses in the passage.

Being a Writer™ • Grade Four

Punctuation and Capitalization: Use colons and semicolons

The Parrot and Mrs. Beardsley: Corrections

A. Corrections are shown below.

Dear Animal Shelter[:]

A parrot arrived on my doorstep at 8:00 PM yesterday. I have never met a bird like it[.] He has extremely bad manners! Has anybody lost a rude bird lately?

Sincerely,

Mrs. Beardsley

B. Conjunctions have been replaced with semicolons in the passage below.

Mrs. Beardsley didn't want to take the bird to the animal shelter[;] ~~because~~ even though the bird had bad manners, it was good company. The parrot and Mrs. Beardsley realized they had many things in common[;] however, Mrs. Beardsley knew that the friendship couldn't last.

The Stand-up: Corrections

A. Corrections are shown below.

Dear Mr. Gooch[:]

I want to become a great stand-up comic. I saw your show last week, and everything about it was amazing[:] your timing, your topics, your facial expressions. So here's my question[:] what do I need to become a successful stand-up comic?

Sincerely,

Gary

B. Conjunctions have been replaced with semicolons in the passage below.

Gary studied other comics[;] ~~and~~ he gathered jokes. He decided to test his act on Alex, his three-year-old brother. Alex found most things funny[;] ~~so~~ Gary should at least get lots of laughs. Even so, the first show with a real audience was a disaster: when Gary walked onstage, the audience pelted him with tomatoes!

Punctuation and Capitalization: Use colons and semicolons

Hiccups: Corrections

A. Corrections are shown below.

Dear Uncle Amit:

This is urgent: how do you stop hiccups? I started

hiccupping at 7:00 p.m. last night, and I'm still going. I've

tried everything; standing on my head, singing, drinking

water backward, and all three at the same time. Do you have

any other ideas?

Hic!

Moshim

B. Conjunctions have been replaced with semicolons in the sentences below.

Moshim thought he would spend the rest of his life

hiccupping. Maybe he would graduate hiccupping; and

he might even get married hiccupping. Then Moshim

remembered Uncle Amit's idea: a scary movie. Moshim

gulped; because just thinking about it was terrifying! His

knees shook; and his skin prickled. Then he realized

The Lost City of Atlantis: Corrections

A. Corrections are shown below.

Dear Travel Agent:

I recently heard about a beautiful city named Atlantis.

At 7:21 AM today, I had the best idea of my life: I'm going to

travel to Atlantis! Therefore, I'd be grateful if you answered

my questions: where exactly is the city located and how much

is a ticket to get there?

Sincerely,

Mrs. A. D. Venturer

B. Conjunctions have been replaced with semicolons in the passage below.

A few days later, Mrs. Venturer learned that Atlantis

might not exist. People had looked for it in many different

places; for example, Antarctica, Indonesia, the Caribbean, and

Ireland. As Mrs. Venturer studied her maps, Bernard the dog

watched her anxiously; because he wanted to go on vacation.

Review: Proofread for grammar, usage, punctuation, and capitalization

The City of the Future: Corrections

A. **Corrections are given below. Some answers may vary.**

What will a city of the future look like? Will it be filled
with traffic, smog, and litter? And will we have to travel for
miles to see a garden or a tree? If we take care of the Earth,
here is what a city of the future might look like. People will
walk, bicycle, or skate to work. However, if they live too far
away, they will take buses or drive cars that run on fuel made
from plants. In the city of the future, there will be trees
everywhere. Old airports and parking lots will be turned into
peaceful parks. After work and on the weekends, people will
walk and breathe the fresh air. In the city of the future, people
will greet one another and smile.

B. **Check for the appropriate use of the practiced skills in the passage.**

Being a Writer™ | **73**

The Zoologist: Corrections

A. **Corrections are given below. Some answers may vary.**

Dian Fossey (1932–1985) loved animals. She trained to
become an animal doctor, but after a trip to Africa, she
decided that the wild mountain gorilla was her passion. She
studied gorillas in Zaire. Later, she started a gorilla study
center in Rwanda. She lived at the center for eighteen years
with the gorillas.

To study the gorillas, Dian first had to gain their trust.
She imitated their habits and sounds. Sometimes, she ate
the same foods that they ate. Slowly, the gorillas began
to trust her, and Dian found that they had personalities just
like people do.

B. **Check for the appropriate use of the practiced skills in the passage.**

74 | Being a Writer™

98 | Being a Writer™ • Grade Four

Review: Proofread for grammar, usage, punctuation, and capitalization

The Loudest Sound in the World: Corrections

A. Corrections are given below. Some answers may vary.

    In 1883, a volcano erupted on the island of Krakatoa in
_I_
indonesia. The explosion (which happened in august) was so
                 _A_
          heard
loud that people in perth, australia, herd it, and people on an
          _P_   _A_
          felt
island 3,000 miles away feel the ground shake.

    The eruption caused huge waves (called tsunamis) to
                    were
crash into nearby islands. Some of the waves were 130
feet
feet high, and they killed many people. Other people was
killed by the hot ash that shot from the volcano. About
three hundred towns and villages disappeared. The island of
        was
Krakatoa were almost completely blown apart.

B. Check for the appropriate use of the practiced skills in the passage.

Being a Writer™ | **75**

How to Save the Earth: Corrections

A. Corrections are given below. Some answers may vary.

_A_
april 22 is Earth Day. Saving the Earth shouldn't be
            one   _are_
limited to won day each year, though! There is lots of small,
                   _do_   _are_
simple things you can does every day. Here is a few ideas:

1. Instead of buying brand new school supplies, use the pens,
pencils, and notebooks that you didn't use up last year.

2. When you wrap a gift, use the pages from old newspapers,
magazines, or comics.

3. Save water by taking a quick shower rather than a bath
you'll get just as clean.

4. To save energy, switch off the lights when you left a room.

      buy   _wrapped_
5. Try to by fruit and vegetables that aren't rapped in plastic.

B. Check for the appropriate use of the practiced skills in the passage.

76 | Being a Writer™

Being a Writer™ • Grade Four | 99

Being a Writer — Reorder Information

Grade 3

Additional Units

Poetry Genre Unit (Teacher's Manual and CD-ROM Reproducible Materials)	BWA-GU3-1
Letter Writing Genre Unit (Teacher's Manual, 2 trade books, and CD-ROM Reproducible Materials)	BWA-GU3-2
Additional Genre Units Package (Poetry Genre Unit and Letter Writing Genre Unit)	BWA-GUP3-1
Preparing for a Writing Test, Grades 3–5 (Teacher's Manual and CD-ROM Reproducible Materials)	BWA-PWT35

Classroom Package — **BW-CP3**

Contents: Teacher's Manual (2 volumes), Skill Practice Teaching Guide, Assessment Resource Book, 25 Student Writing Handbooks, 25 Student Skill Practice Books, and 33 trade books.

Available separately

Teacher's Manual, vol. 1	BW-TM3-V1
Teacher's Manual, vol. 2	BW-TM3-V2
Skill Practice Teaching Guide	BW-STG3
Assessment Resource Book	BW-AB3
Student Writing Handbook pack (5 books)	BW-SB3-Q5
Student Skill Practice Book pack (5 books)	BW-SSB3-Q5
CD-ROM Grade 3 Reproducible Materials	BW-CDR3
Trade book set (33 books)	BW-TBS3

Grade 4

Additional Units

Persuasive Nonfiction Genre Unit (Teacher's Manual and CD-ROM Reproducible Materials)	BWA-GU4-1
Letter Writing Genre Unit (Teacher's Manual and CD-ROM Reproducible Materials)	BWA-GU4-2
Additional Genre Units Package (Persuasive Nonfiction Genre Unit and Letter Writing Genre Unit)	BWA-GUP4-1
Preparing for a Writing Test, Grades 3–5 (Teacher's Manual and CD-ROM Reproducible Materials)	BWA-PWT35

Classroom Package — **BW-CP4**

Contents: Teacher's Manual (2 volumes), Skill Practice Teaching Guide, Assessment Resource Book, 30 Student Writing Handbooks, 30 Student Skill Practice Books, and 25 trade books.

Available separately

Teacher's Manual, vol. 1	BW-TM4-V1
Teacher's Manual, vol. 2	BW-TM4-V2
Skill Practice Teaching Guide	BW-STG4
Assessment Resource Book	BW-AB4
Student Writing Handbook pack (5 books)	BW-SB4-Q5
Student Skill Practice Book pack (5 books)	BW-SSB4-Q5
CD-ROM Grade 4 Reproducible Materials	BW-CDR4
Trade book set (25 books)	BW-TBS4

Grade 5

Additional Units

Letter Writing Genre Unit (Teacher's Manual, 1 trade book, and CD-ROM Reproducible Materials)	BWA-GU5-1
Functional Writing Genre Unit (Teacher's Manual and CD-ROM Reproducible Materials)	BWA-GU5-2
Additional Genre Units Package (Letter Writing Genre Unit and Functional Writing Genre Unit)	BWA-GUP5-1
Preparing for a Writing Test, Grades 3–5 (Teacher's Manual and CD-ROM Reproducible Materials)	BWA-PWT35

Classroom Package — **BW-CP5**

Contents: Teacher's Manual (2 volumes), Skill Practice Teaching Guide, Assessment Resource Book, 30 Student Writing Handbooks, 30 Student Skill Practice Books, and 25 trade books.

Available separately

Teacher's Manual, vol. 1	BW-TM5-V1
Teacher's Manual, vol. 2	BW-TM5-V2
Skill Practice Teaching Guide	BW-STG5
Assessment Resource Book	BW-AB5
Student Writing Handbook pack (5 books)	BW-SB5-Q5
Student Skill Practice Book pack (5 books)	BW-SSB5-Q5
CD-ROM Grade 5 Reproducible Materials	BW-CDR5
Trade book set (25 books)	BW-TBS5

Grade 6

Additional Units

Letter Writing Genre Unit (Teacher's Manual, 1 trade book, and CD-ROM Reproducible Materials)	BWA-GU6-1
Functional Writing Genre Unit (Teacher's Manual, 1 trade book, and CD-ROM Reproducible Materials)	BWA-GU6-2
Additional Genre Units Package (Letter Writing Genre Unit and Functional Writing Genre Unit)	BWA-GUP6-1

Classroom Package — **BW-CP6**

Contents: Teacher's Manual (2 volumes), Skill Practice Teaching Guide, Assessment Resource Book, 30 Student Writing Handbooks (2 volumes), 30 Student Skill Practice Books, and 14 trade books.

Available separately

Teacher's Manual, vol. 1	BW-TM6-V1
Teacher's Manual, vol. 2	BW-TM6-V2
Skill Practice Teaching Guide	BW-STG6
Assessment Resource Book	BW-AB6
Student Writing Handbook pack (5 books)	BW-SB6-Q5
Student Skill Practice Book pack (5 books)	BW-SSB6-Q5
CD-ROM Grade 6 Reproducible Materials	BW-CDR6
Trade book set (14 books)	BW-TBS6

The *Being a Writer* program is also available at grades K–2. Visit www.devstu.org for more information.

Ordering Information:

To order call 800.666.7270 * fax 510.842.0348 * log on to www.devstu.org * e-mail pubs@devstu.org

Or Mail Your Order to:

Developmental Studies Center * Publications Department * 2000 Embarcadero, Suite 305 * Oakland, CA 94606-5300

DEVELOPMENTAL STUDIES CENTER